SUNSET

Sunset

SUNSET

ON THE *Passing* OF THOSE WE *Love*

S. MICHAEL WILCOX

**DESERET
BOOK**

Salt Lake City, Utah

Library of Congress Cataloging-in-Publication Data
Wilcox, S. Michael, author.
   Sunset : on the passing of those we love / S. Michael Wilcox.
      pages cm
   Includes bibliographical references.
   ISBN 978-1-60908-834-7 (hardbound : alk. paper)
   1. Death—Religious aspects—Church of Jesus Christ of Latter-day Saints.
2. Bereavement—Religious aspects—Church of Jesus Christ of Latter-day Saints.
3. Church of Jesus Christ of Latter-day Saints—Doctrines. I. Title.
   BX8643.D4W55 2011
   236'.1—dc23   2011037883

Printed in the United States of America
R. R. Donnelley, Crawfordsville, IN

10   9   8   7   6

To all those friends in the garden
who watched and prayed with us
—and did not sleep.

✥

"Blessed are they that mourn:
for they shall be comforted."
—*Matthew 5:4*

We pray for comfort from pain, Father,
not the lessening of the love that causes it.

CONTENTS

RELEASE

Take . . . these thoughts which here unfolded too,
And which on warm and cold days I withdrew
From my heart's ground . . .
Sonnet Forty-Four

A Personal Journey

I did not know I had so many tears. I have tried to hide most of them. Not that I am ashamed of tears, but seeing them in my eyes brings them too often to the cheeks of others, and I would not spread sorrow too widely. Yet there is a cleansing of the soul through the eyes. Tears release sadness that must not dominate, leaving only love, somewhat older, wiser, calmer, and yet renewed, reborn, freshened, enlarged, flowering. The soul was not made by God to be sorrow's home. He would have us happy. We open the doors and windows and let sorrow out. We learn from the memory of its visits, then let the breezes of continued living clear the air. We learn to breathe again, to walk in the sunlight. Love, joy, peace, each other are the true inhabitants, and we would not crowd them unnecessarily.

I wrote the above shortly after my wife's passing. Writing has become, with the tears, my release. To be honest, I am trying to survive, as well as to learn from those dream-breaking moments. There has been a continent shift in my life that will be understood by many who have been where I am. Grief is love's shadow. It is cast over me now by the loss of Laurie, but it need not block the sunlight. That light is always shining above the clouds somewhere, and though I cannot currently feel its rays, I assume she can, and there is comfort in that.

I am trying to learn death's lessons, and surely one of them is how much life is a gift, one we cannot treasure too closely. There is too much of the divine in it. Often, in the night, I have listened for hours to Laurie's labored breathing next to me. What a wonderful thing it is to draw another breath. King Benjamin once reminded his people to be grateful to God who is "preserving you from day to day, by lending you breath" (Mosiah 2:21). Why did he use the verb *lending*? I wonder.

These have been days of pain but also of profound love and gratitude. I have kept a small notebook near me during the last weeks and months wherein I have tried to record what I was learning about living and loving and grieving. I did not initially intend it for publication, but somewhere along the journey I was reminded that we are under divine injunction and sacred covenant to share our burdens, our mourning, our comforts, and our witnesses. To that end, and by way of tribute to the woman I love, I offer my own passage, desiring that it may lift others who share the path with me or who will one day find themselves on the same road hoping someone left a few signposts to help them find their way. I have not aimed at chronology or organizational order in my thoughts, for they did not arrive from life that way—and to be truthful I am still trying to make sense of all that has passed throughout the last months.

I am taking my first footsteps in grief's journey through the changing landscape of my life without Laurie. Perhaps to call it an odyssey would be more descriptive, for that word suggests a predetermined direction, and there is no doubt in the desired ending place. In the Greek classic, Odysseus bent all his efforts, which were arduous and occupied years, toward returning to the love of Penelope and Telemachus, his wife and son, whom he left behind when he went to the Trojan wars. His multiple endeavors were in time bounteously rewarded with a homecoming rooted in the lasting and continued love of both wife and child. That welcome more than recompensed him for the obstacles he had encountered and the loneliness he had endured. Separation sends us on our own personal journey, ever yearning for those from whom we have parted. Grief is a searching, desiring emotion. It is the heart's hunger—the soul reaching out, stretching itself beyond mortality's boundaries. We do not merely miss the departed, we long for them, deeply, as Odysseus longed for Penelope. Yet, are we not assured by the promises of our own hearts, as well as those of the gospel, that the homecoming will be worth the paths we have walked, no matter how long or how difficult the road may have been? I am beginning that odyssey.

ELIZABETH BARRETT AND ROBERT BROWNING

Laurie and I both enjoyed, and related to, the exchanges of affection between Elizabeth Barrett and Robert Browning.

The quotations that precede each chapter are all taken from *Sonnets from the Portuguese* written by Elizabeth to Robert, who had come to associate Elizabeth with her Portuguese heroine, Catarina, from one of her earlier poems. "Keep my ribbon, take and keep it. I have loosed it from my hair," Catarina wrote to the man who loved her upon her death so he would remember her. Aside from the sentiments included in the sonnets, which seem to fit so perfectly, Laurie's long hair was something we both delighted in; I thought the inclusions were appropriate and would please her.

Elizabeth died many years before Robert. I had no idea until Laurie's cancer and eventual passing how important the Brownings' expressions of love for each other would become. We admired and enjoyed them before; they have become critical supports to me now. Shortly after Elizabeth's death, Robert penned into her testament the words written by Dante about Beatrice, the woman he loved, who had also died young. I have quoted them to myself more times than I could relate as their increasing ascent of confidence and conviction from belief to certainty helps to light the candle of my own faith when sorrow's curtains close in and the twilight of doubt descends.

> *Thus I believe,*
> *Thus I affirm,*
> *Thus I am certain it is,*
> *That from this life I shall pass to another.*
> *There, where that lady lives*
> *Of whom my soul was enamored.*

DANTE, CONVITO, II:9

CHAPTER I

THE ETERNAL REACH

. . . The widest Land
Doom takes to part us leaves thy heart in mine
With pulses that beat double. What I do
And what I dream include thee . . .

Sonnet Six

The Gordian Knot

There is a story told of Alexander the Great while he was on his way to conquering the known world. He faced the puzzle of the Gordian knot, a tangle of rope so complicated that no one could untie it. I remember visualizing this knot when young, wondering in my imagination if I could have succeeded better than the great Alexander. There were no ends seen to the knot as the rope twisted and turned upon itself, hiding the beginning and the end within the interior mass of the fibers. Alexander failed, and in a final act of frustration this man of action drew his sword and sliced through the rope, severing its coils and scattering them on the ground. He could conquer the world, defeat the mighty Persian Empire, but was defeated himself by the mystery of entwining cords.

I have thought of this story over the last months as I have tried to endure the dying of my wife, Laurie. My thoughts turn upon themselves and I cannot find a beginning and ending, a way through. My emotions are so varied and changing, sometimes within seconds. Fear, doubt, love, grief, empathy, longing, hope, acceptance, denial, faith all find their place in the turnings of my mind. Then there are the questions—above all the questions. There is also the physical element of grief, which reminds me of nightmares I had as a boy when panic would grip my stomach, wash upward into my chest, and hold me motionless in the darkness. Grief feels like that sometimes. It hurts, physically hurts. It is a constricting, suffocating pain. At the emotional-physical level it is first cousin to being terrified.

I am grateful that anger at God has not as yet found a place in my tangle of feelings, but I can understand how it could. Perhaps that is the first great lesson I am learning: that God can take our most precious thing, can allow the severing of a part of ourselves, and we can still love and trust Him. But is He taking her, as if it were some part of His plan? We speak in these terms so commonly, but I doubt He is.

I don't think there is a determined time for each of us to go. Life happens, and even God shares our sorrow at its ability to stun us, but He has a much larger perspective. I think He would say to us, "Laurie and Mike, I'm sorry this terrible thing has happened. I wish you could have those many future years you dreamed of sharing, but I cannot save everyone whom cancer has appointed to die. The hollow your grief creates I will one day fill with joy. Everything will pass and all will be well." Does the scriptural phrase "appointed unto death" (Doctrine and Covenants 42:48) mean God has decided "our time to go," or has life brought its own unwelcomed conclusions? At any rate, we are promised that "God shall wipe away all tears from their eyes; and there shall be no more death, neither sorrow, nor crying, neither shall there be any more pain: for the former things are passed away" (Revelation 21:4).

Sometimes the rush of emotions becomes so constant it feels like there is not enough air in the world to draw in and contain them from spilling out, usually in the form of tears. I have to breathe deeply to stay in control. How can I make sense of them all? We are all grieving in our own ways—one daughter in her need for her mother, another in the painful memories of those last weeks, the boys in a certain quiet, numbing puzzlement, and me in my nervous anxieties, ceaseless internal discussions, and relentless longing for my perfected Laurie of a thousand combined memories. It is all sometimes so confusing. I was so used to being in control, knowing what I wanted and where I was going. There were few ambiguities, and certitude was my expectation. Much is being challenged. Now my uncertainties seem to pull the knot into an unyielding tension.

The more one wrestled to untie the Gordian knot, the tighter it became and the less yielding of its secret. Watching one you love pass through the struggle of ending life is like that. You feel lost in a maze of emotions, sentiments, and turmoil, and there is no Ariadne to hand you the clue of thread to find your way out of the labyrinth.

And what of Laurie's thoughts? They must matter more than mine, yet of them I was largely ignorant. Hers I did not really know, though I could guess them, for the cancer had stopped her ability to communicate. But even if it had not silenced her speech, she was not one who opened her mind easily. The thought that she was dying was too threatening for her. She turned from it. I do not believe it was the fear of the unknown that troubled her. She just wanted to live; "living is so dear" (Thoreau, *Walden*, 81). So we survived day by day without her expressing what she was feeling and thinking.

ONE WITH HUMANITY

I will write—but not from my head primarily, as always in the past—for writing seems to bring with it a clarifying and ordering of my thoughts and my faith, and there is a renewing. Perhaps it will do the same with emotions. God has so often filled my mind with His truth while I was writing; surely He will do so now at the level of the soul. I write for my own peace and solace, but also in the hope that those who face the passing of their own dear ones and labor to make sense of it, to wrap their hearts and souls and minds and future lives around it, may possibly find some measure of understanding through a shared experience. My life had been so comfortable. Things I had once called trials seem so minimal now. Perhaps the graciousness of the life God had allotted me had separated me too much from the majority of my fellow men. I thought I could empathize with them, had empathized with them. Now I think, "So this is what so many for so long have endured!"

There is healing in the flow and ripple of words. Both grief and love must be expressed somehow, someway—grief that it may lessen or at least become endurable, and love because to speak it, to share it, to open the heart, intensifies it and increases it, lets it grow out in the open air and light. Unexpressed love dies, suffocating in the confining, restricted space of the self. One thing I believe above all else: Laurie's early death has taught me a great deal about loving and being loved. All of love's expressions—affection and romance, the spiritual and the physical, the emotional and the familial, its quiet acceptance and its passionate yearning for otherness, learning and sharing, forgiving and sacrificing, woman and wife, intimate lover and devoted friend, the needed and searched-for help—meet for all dimensions of a joined life. Did she realize how much she took with her in her passing? Do I yet realize it? Do we feel how much life was filled until the emptiness left teaches us its volume? Yet the loving remains and grows and is itself a kind of filling. Death breaks the heart, but in living, most of the deepest sorrow seeps out through the cracks until love can seal them and replenish the hollowed-out spaces. But the heart remains touch-tender—and oh, the little things the magnet of our longing is drawn toward.

Someone asked me, "What do you miss most?"

"Holding hands while walking; feeling her fingers on my arm; her insistence that I always stand one step down to compensate for our difference in height; calling her 'little one'; her voice singing *Mary's Lullaby*; sensing her smile on my face when I'm not looking; seeing love in her eyes," I answered, and then turned away as a hundred other tiny "everythings" flooded back.

The Backward Yearning

When it became apparent that we could not win the battle against the cancer, Laurie's mother asked what she could do for me. I told her I wanted the picture of Laurie that used to sit on the piano in their home in Alberta. She was almost eighteen, her age when I first met her. I remember the first time I saw that picture. Laurie and I were dating, and I had driven with her to Canada to attend her sister's wedding and to meet her family. Somehow the turning of her head, the downward flow of her hair, the simplicity of her smile, and the open lighting of her eyes caught some essence about her. It was pure Laurie captive in time. I had coveted that picture for almost forty years, so I asked my mother-in-law if I could now have it. She brought it to Utah with her, along with many other photographs of Laurie as a child growing up.

I realized as I turned through the pages of her past that I loved her at every age. Though I had not met her until she was a freshman in college, I fell in love with the five-year-old in curls and ribbons, the ten-year-old vacationing in Waterton Park, the fifteen-year-old high school student walking through the snow of Alberta with her books. I had seen these pictures before, they were not new to me, but as I went through her past I realized a new dimension of eternal love.

We speak of the everlasting nature of love, its infinite scope (only Mormons truly believe all the love songs and have as their most sacred ordinance the verification of that belief). I always imagined that ceaseless, eternal love as stretching down the long corridor of welcoming time, past horizons, past setting suns and turning galaxies, but my vision was always a future one, of time unspent. Now I feel it pulling me backwards, through every moment of her childhood, her growing preparatory years, the seasons of dolls and dances, first lipstick and earrings, times that I did not share with her but that were now as precious as if I had always known her, always loved her, had never lived without her. And I sense in this backward yearning that when the day comes that veils and closed doors will part and open, the reach of love will encompass all the eons of the past so that eventually there will never be a time when I did not love her.

I am not speaking of the commonly held—with just a touch of Mormon folklore—belief that we knew and loved each other in a premortal life. It is not that! But something deeper, more holy, first created, initially begun, in the temple, at the altar, there where the eternal motion toward both future and past begins its infinite longing reach.

15

I look through the chaining chambers of reflected eternity in temple mirrors differently now. She is in each reflection: those that stretch before me with such promise and those that reach comfortably behind me like a familiar landscape or the peace of going home. Was she ever not there? Was there ever a time I did not love her? No, it seems in this that love is retrospective and captures all the moments of the past and makes them part of the now, one eternal round, all things in the present, time in perfect wholeness, union before union. Ironically it is death, the perceived ender of things, that has given me this gift of enhanced ages. Shakespeare spoke of "love-devouring death," but would not the proper name be love-engendering death?

CHAPTER II

"ALL THAT GOLDEN GOODNESS"

If I leave all for thee, wilt thou exchange
And be all to me?

Sonnet Thirty-Five

. . . from out thee overcame
My soul with satisfaction of all wants—
Because God's gifts put man's best dreams to shame.

Sonnet Twenty-Six

ENDEARMENTS

*T*he past is a wonder of remembrance, a place we must go but not linger too long in some of its environments. Like all couples, we had our disagreements, those dark times that could dim the light of feeling. These were the moments when we mutually agreed that I was insensitive and that she overreacted. It was a good way to describe things, and the humor in it muted the edges of our disappointment in each other. Among all the positives, there were some negatives, which sprang from the weaknesses, pride, and follies of us both. I suppose all marriages embrace some painful memories. I distrust those who maintain they've never known these things. They tap the springs of my guilt. Are they not part of frail and flawed mankind? "I should have been a better husband," comes to mind more times than I can sometimes bear. And with that thought, the doubts and fears loom larger than shadows. They begin to take on the solidity of reality. I think all people who suffer the loss of a loved one, especially a spouse, pass through dark doubts; at least in the last months almost all I have talked to have expressed a similar uneasiness to a greater or lesser extent. In spite of temple covenants, in spite of my faith in eternity, I cannot help but question if she will still want me. "She will!" I'm always told by those who knew us best, but black doubts when I am alone with my fears are not easily dismissed. Without her I can conceive of no lasting eternal happiness. If I cannot be with her, it will not matter what God gives me—I will have missed heaven. Yet some assuring voice inside says it wouldn't have been love if it went away because of our weaknesses.

She often worried about her own imperfections and inadequacies, but how unimportant they all are now. Little annoyances have suddenly become endearments. How I miss not seeing her morning necessities—the lotions, lipsticks, eye shadows, blush, curling irons, combs, hairbrushes—scattered across the bathroom counter, forever encroaching on my side and spilling into the drawers below. These she always shut just before her exit, whereupon she would sweep down the stairs, past where I sat waiting for her on the couch, and into the car. Thus it was always me that made us late as I scrambled after her out the door with a brief pause to slip on my shoes. How come I wasn't ready? For justification she would quote her mother, "Any old barn looks better with a fresh coat of paint!" But out of that chaos of makeup and hair dryers, the feminine face I most loved appeared new each day.

I could never get her to come to bed at night, as she preferred reading in a chair. "You'll just go to sleep," I'd say, "and be in the chair all night." "No, I'll come to bed in a few minutes." Night after night, at two or three in the morning, I would find her fast asleep in the chair, book opened to the place it had been when I had last talked with her and the lights burning. Almost every book she read has faint little wandering, scratching pen marks on its pages. "Here's where she fell asleep," I would say when reading the same book later. All so endearing now!

She lost at least one half of every pair of earrings she ever owned—and she would never go out in public without them. She loved bracelets and must have bought at least a hundred in the last few years. I used to question why she needed another one, but the sight of all her bracelets and single earrings in the drawer brought such warmth to my heart the other day that I would not have cared had she purchased a thousand. I could not help but buy her one last bracelet and place it on her, along with a tiny set of pearl earrings—the final thing I did before she was buried. She would not have wanted to go into the Lord's presence without a bracelet and earrings. Endearments!

So love reaches back into the past and turns all the droughts to watered gardens. Now none of the negatives matter, the sting of words nor the thoughtlessness of deeds. Past pain is forgotten. Her loving me in all my humanness, and I her, melts the weaknesses away for both of us, like the quick blowing out of a candle until even the tiniest wisps of smoke dissipate in the air. We say to one another our favorite line from Shakespeare—the brief, beautiful, forgiving words Cordelia said with such tenderness to King Lear, her father, who had so wronged her and feared he had given her ample cause for permanent alienation: "No cause, no cause." If I pass through the veil and see her waiting, only the sweetness will remain; all the rest will have disappeared in a forgiving, forgetting blink of time, like a breeze fanning away the heat or the flow of warm air taking the chill off our face. It will be that easy. Yet there are times I cannot get beyond the fears of that "if." I could have done so many things so much better. Did I cherish her enough? Was I nourishing? However, I tell myself that God would not continue to let me hurt without healing if Laurie were lost to me forever. No good God could possibly do that. He would begin to take her out of my heart. The fact that she remains locked within so tightly and that the ache continues at such a high level should tell me she is still mine and I hers, and I need not worry. "No cause, no cause."

THE ALTARS OF THE TEMPLE

*W*e must not allow our fears, or our grief, or our doubts to destroy our hope or take away the brightness of the future. How often have I imparted those words to friends and students in their spiritual wrestlings? Can I believe them now with the same calm assurance with which I offered them to others? God has not answered many a prayer these last months and weeks as I would have desired, and sometimes the silences have left me with anxious wondering, but He has frequently pressed into my soul certain assurances I try not to allow my restless disquiet to dismiss.

I find Him drawing my thoughts back to the days when we first met and grew into love—as if those days gave us the truest sight of each other, in spite of all their romantic colorings, for there was nothing but perfection in all I saw. We should love people for what they are at their very best, the totality of all their highest moments from every age. This is the real person, the eternal one, the one we are to remember and hold dear, I of her and she of me. Death insists upon this vision. Throughout our lives together, whenever I looked through the oh-so-very-thin veil of her limitations with my most loving, my purest, my most exalted eyes and saw her as she was—beautiful, gentle, warm, loving, the perfection of refined femininity—then I was looking at the true Laurie.

The scriptures speak of being faithful to "the wife of thy youth" and "the wife of thy covenant" (Malachi 2:14). Laurie will always be eighteen to me, the bride of my youth. That is the girl I hold in my heart and will always hold there. I will not, must not, harbor in the closets of my mind those anguish-filled memories of what pain and cancer did to her. Too much joy-lifting life overflows them, washing the mind clean. To those first fondly contemplated images is added the multitude of memories of her presence in hundreds of different situations at every age, yet there is something about that earliest picture that nothing else can overpower. In the final reuniting when we greet each other with, "My own beloved!" she will be more her true self than ever I knew of her in life, for the nobler we are, the more completely we reflect the perfections of Him in whose image we are created both inside and out.

My life has been filled with many wonderful and happy moments, but there is one that has for decades remained the single most defining and joyful instant of my life, and to this sliver of time the Lord directs my memory. It was that July day in 1972 when I knelt at the altar in the Cardston Alberta Temple and looked across it into Laurie's face. I believe God opened the windows of His celestial world for just enough time for a ray of glory and light and love to flood down upon us. I have never been able to adequately describe that brief blink of eternity, but as C. S. Lewis once wrote, "Such a sweetness and power rolled about them and over them and entered them that they felt they had never really been happy or wise or good, or even alive and awake, before. And the memory of that moment stayed with them always, so that as long as they both lived, if ever they were sad or afraid or angry, the thought of all that golden goodness, and the feeling that it was still there, quite close, just round some corner or just behind some door, would come back and make them sure, deep down inside, that all was well" (*The Magician's Nephew*, 161). That is how I have looked on our sealing that July day. That is the comfort eternal covenants impart. That is a power beyond cancer, beyond separation, beyond even the lonely longing that looks ahead to the years when I will not hear her voice, or see her face, or feel her touch. It was the happiest day of my life, and its remembered joy continues to be a fulfillment that outweighs any price life may exact from me in the form of pain or adversity. I have *that day*, and no amount of suffering or remorse can deny me of its solace. If she loves me, I am in heaven already, and life can do what it will.

"WE'LL HAVE ALL ETERNITY"

There is deeper listening than that allowed the ears, and touches of the spirit are the most gentle. These I pray the Lord will allow her to give me from time to time while I wait for reunion. I think what bothered us both as the reality of her shortened life continued to dawn upon us was how much we would miss of what we had planned and looked forward to doing. I had retired early—a mere three months before the seizures came that announced the growing tumor in her brain—specifically to spend more time with her. When people would ask me why I was retiring so soon, I would tell them, "Because I do not want anything to happen to either Laurie or me to cut short the time I want to spend with her. Five more years of work may compromise all we want to do." I had just been released from ten years in the stake presidency the previous December and so enjoyed sitting every Sunday in church with her. I wanted to assure her she was first in my life, above teaching the scriptures, above speaking assignments or leadership calls, above writing books, or directing tours, or even raising children.

After her passing, I found in her dresser drawer the letter I had written to her on our thirty-third wedding anniversary. McKay, our last son, was on his mission and there were just the two of us in the house.

> "The wheel has turned its full rotation and once again we are alone. Perhaps, it is a fault in me, but I have longed for the years that lie ahead. 'Joy and rejoicing' have truly been the heritage our children shaped for us, and the sweetness of the 'Daddy' days will linger forever in my memory, but I feel the tug of eternity—voices echoing among the stars which promise a journey to distant places beyond the scope of our greatest imaginations—and I want to prepare for it; to share it with my bride . . ."

Through the years, she supported me and waited. It was her time, our time. We had all the countries laid out we wanted to see—the natural wonders as well as man's highest achievements. I had just given her a map of the earth to fill with pins, telling her triumphantly, "I'll give you the world!" As I looked at her lying in the hospice bed, it was hard to believe that this woman who loved so freely the countries and peoples of the world, who visited all seven continents and traveled so widely, should now be reduced to the limiting space of a narrow bed; and even there she had not freedom of movement, as the cancer began to lock her muscles into permanent motionlessness.

Our last tour together was to Peru. When we first took a group there several years ago and fell in love with the Andes, the people, and the Inca ruins, we vowed we would return with our children if we had to do it one by one. We brought three of them and our daughter-in-law with us on this final trip. I reminded Laurie of our desire, and that it was more than half fulfilled. "Yes," she said, then, struggling to find the words through the confusion the cancer was spreading slowly through her brain, she whispered so softly I could barely hear, "I wanted to . . . twenty years." These are moments of poignancy I offer to my God with each questioning, "Why?"

One evening just days after she died, the sadness became so overwhelming, I cried out to the Lord, "Could you not have given us the twenty years we anticipated, the twenty she wanted? Could you not have given us ten? Or just five? Or even a mere two?" There was no bitterness in my voice—that would have been relieving—just despair. And I heard her voice deep down in the depths of being where only the most needed of answers calm. "We'll have all eternity." Four simple words—how I love the altars of the temple!

As Necessary as the Altar

I think a great part of the pain we feel when those we love pass through the veil is the ache that comes with thinking of all we wished we could share with them. All of life, a hundred years of it, a thousand, would not be sufficient to enjoy, we finally realize. Life granted me only thirty-eight years with her. Not enough! There is so much gladness to share, so much to experience and learn, so much good to accomplish. Yet nothing is completely lost, only postponed for a time. I'll have "all eternity" to be with Laurie, and it will be so much better for the fervent, lonely yearning of separation, even though it stretches for the years or remaining decades of my life. I will always remember that ache, and it will one day sanctify and fill with gratitude a future reunion. Traces of that mourning will remain, but now made holy by the surmounting joy—a joy that could, perhaps, not reach so high without the sorrow it replaces. Perhaps separation must be a part of all eternal marriages, be that time long or short. Even those for whom it is short will feel the hunger I feel, one that cannot be satisfied on earth. Whether long or short, the intensity of the first moments and days and weeks is enough. And I assume those in the spirit world feel the division, the leave-taking, too. Maybe Laurie is saying this very moment, "I wish Mike were here." But the sting of longing must be less there than here—at least the scriptures lead us to think that way. Yet longing is longing.

It may be that all those who love need some period of partition or farewell and the pains it brings. Grieving may be as much a part of loving as courting, or forgiving, or embracing, or sharing—the grave as crucial a necessity as the altar in sanctifying love. Did not the writer of Ecclesiastes say there was a time and season for everything, "a time to every purpose under the heaven"? (Ecclesiastes 3:1). *Purpose* is such a deliberate word. So there must be a purpose to dying beyond just getting out of mortality. Surely that purpose has to do with uniting souls for all of life, urging us to oneness.

On that scriptural list in Ecclesiastes were "a time to weep . . . to mourn . . . to embrace . . . to refrain from embracing . . . to lose . . . to love." There was also a time "to die." They are all connected. If I cherish the glad memory of the altar, can I reject the tears at the ending? *Ending* is not the right word. Laurie's passing was not the last phase of our marriage, just another step in the eternal dance.

> *"Is that true, Lord? Is this ache within me part of Thy greater wisdom?"*

I want her to be happy; I sense she is. And she would want me to be happy, but would we not both add, "But not totally, not yet, not until we're together." What life may not have taught me thoroughly enough—that I need her for my happiness, that she is all that really matters, that she was the best gift God ever gave me—death has taught. He is a most efficient instructor. But did the lesson have to come so soon?

I have thought about the "times" within our marriage, the life stages, times that do not fade away as a new period is entered but blend and welcome the new age. They never made the Ecclesiastes list but were, perhaps, encased in its simple, "a time to love." There was the time of romance and passion in those innocent, dream-driven, early blissful years. Then the children came, and I watched the selfless mother live for her daughters and sons. This was the time of gratitude and admiration, which bloomed in our love, but the family years passed more quickly than either of us could have imagined. As the children leaned into their own lives and worlds and the home emptied, it was the time of friendship and sharing, the rediscovery of ourselves, personality not measured in hours of homework, Cub Scout badges, or prom dresses. But we will miss the twilight, the evening years, the time of affection and endearment that comes with whitened hair and wrinkled faces, the slow walking time that sees the passing scenery of life again with the wonder of childhood because the details are savored and more fully appreciated. Is there also a time to be alone? Or is it a time to wait? What will the waiting create? What will the aloneness bring? Toward what destination do we strive?

THE CELESTIAL KINGDOM

I was once pondering and reflecting on the celestial kingdom. I do not remember the context, but the Spirit seemed to ask me if I would like to see it. I did not know how to answer that prompting, so I replied I would love to see it if my Father in Heaven was pleased to show it to me. He was. I thought I would see great wonders of nature magnified a thousand times above the beauty of earth's splendors. I thought I would see those many mansions spoken of by Jesus at the Last Supper—far beyond the architectural gems of man's imagination. I pictured flowered gardens and horizons that stretched past sweeping green landscapes to sapphire skies radiant with stars. But He showed me a woman. She was dressed in light, with her long hair sweeping down across her shoulders as white as anything I could imagine. Warmth, and purity, and love, and joy flowed from her, and her green eyes looked upon me with peace and devotion. Her smile was mild and calm and welcoming. God showed me my wife, my Laurie. In that moment, which lives to this day in my imagination, I learned that the celestial reward is not so much a place as it is a person, not merely an environment of brilliance and grandeur but a relationship—the sealing of souls. It is love. And once in my mortal life, at an altar in a temple in Alberta, Canada, I felt it, saw it, knew it in the face and smile of an eighteen-year-old girl who simply said, "Yes," as God blended our souls in preparation for eternity. Is this not the final destination to which love directs us? A time for oneness! It is so heartening to put that my in front of Laurie's name—only one woman to receive that personal title. And I will be hers in equal kind. Then, if God smiles upon us, what greater blessedness could we ever hope for? That is the glory we travel toward. In the scriptures, we have been promised all that the Father hath. Is this because He gives us the highest blessing, and to have the highest is to have everything beneath? The summit commands all that is spread below, all the plains, valleys, and the mountain too from the peak—all things given in the one great gift. Again I say, "How I love the altars of the temple!"

CHAPTER III

FEAR DEATH?

. . . Oh, to shoot
My soul's full meaning into future years
That they should lend it utterance, and salute
Love that endures, from Life that disappears.

Sonnet Forty-One

PREMONITIONS AND REALITY

*W*hen I was young I never feared death—I never thought of it, actually, because it was too far away. Though I knew life was a gift, and a precious one, the thought that it would be taken away was simply beyond the scope of my experience. As I have grown older and seen friends and family members die—sometimes slowly, with months of advance notice, as it was with Laurie, and sometimes with sudden rapidity that stuns the soul—death has pressed itself more keenly upon my conscious thoughts. If I could choose my own passing I am not sure which I would hope for. They are both equally difficult to face, and each leaves a mark on the hearts of those who remain and those who go. I have feared (or, perhaps, respected) death more in my later years. I have wished and even prayed for a long life. Life has so much to give, and I believe I was born with a hunger to harvest the whole crop, to thresh it out and cherish every grain and kernel. Death was something to be avoided. I find now a great paradox in my feelings about dying. It is that love brings and takes away the fear of death, makes it both foe and friend.

My journey began on April 24, 2010. I was in Pittsburgh speaking for Deseret Book's Time Out for Women. I would only be gone for a night. Throughout our married life, I had many times left Laurie home while I traveled for speaking engagements. We were both used to it. She always wanted me to go and share with the Saints what insights the Lord had granted me. I received an emergency phone call while in Atlanta boarding a connecting flight to Salt Lake City. The message was unclear. I was trying to make contact with someone at home as the plane was waiting to taxi. The stewardess asked if I needed to get off. I said, "NO," knowing that whatever emergency awaited, it was in Salt Lake. I flew home not knowing what urgent need I would face when we landed.

It was a long four-hour flight as I was left to my thoughts. I had the distinct feeling pressed upon me by the Spirit that my life was about to change dramatically. I did not know if a child or my wife was the center of the emergency. My son had been rock climbing in Moab, and I feared he had fallen. All sorts of anxious thoughts pass through the mind during such a crisis, and I found myself praying—pleading, really—with the Lord, "Please don't let it be anything to do with the brain, anything but that!" Laurie and I had both expressed earlier in our lives the fear that one of us would have a brain injury or a stroke, and neither wanted it for the other. I felt somewhat guilty that I was praying such, as if we could pick and choose our trials, when the Spirit whispered, "Even Jesus once prayed that a bitter cup would pass from him." No prayers are improper.

I suppose my foreboding was augmented by the disturbing memory of a dream, a nightmare in truth, I had recently had. In the dream, Laurie and I were much younger, enjoying being together in a foreign country. She was running ahead of me and I was chasing her, trying to catch up. We were both laughing and looking forward to a relaxing evening alone together. As she approached the stairway of the hotel, she looked back momentarily to see if I was still following and tripped on the top stair. I watched her fall, just out of my reach to steady her, and strike her head on the post at the bottom. She cried out my name once. I rushed down the stairs and gathered her into my arms. She never spoke again and died a few minutes later of brain trauma with me pleading, "Don't take my wife, Father! Please, please, don't take my wife!"

I have never dismissed a dream. I didn't tell Laurie about it, but it had haunted me for months. I was also disturbed by a song Hilary Weeks had been singing as part of her presentation for Time Out. It was a lovely song she had composed, titled, "If I Only Had Today." It tells of the things one would do if he or she only had one more day to share with a loved one. Over the last few weeks I had not been able to get it out of my mind, hearing it played over and over again along the same grooves of my thoughts. I would wake up hearing it and try to shut it out at night so I could go to sleep. Hilary had sung it that morning. I had just asked her who she was thinking of when she sang it—her husband or her children? She answered, "My family." I anticipated such an answer and did not tell her that I could only think of Laurie when I heard it.

The four hours dragged on as I dealt with my premonitions, those intimations of a coming change. When we landed I received a text message that I was to call my daughter. I soon heard Kirsten's voice. She was at the hospital, and Laurie had a mass of some sort on her brain. Kirsten had found her mother at home on the floor amid knocked-over furniture and tangled in the bedding. She had been alone at home in an almost constant state of seizure for over twenty-four hours.

The words of Job rose in my mind, "For the thing which I greatly feared is come upon me" (Job 3:25).

Within a half an hour I walked into the intensive care unit. The tumor and swelling in Laurie's brain had stopped her ability to speak. She was weak, couldn't walk, and had pneumonia from aspirating the fluids of her stomach due to the nausea caused by the seizures. Nothing she said made any sense to us, but she smiled at me as I walked in. I thought, *I will never talk with her again.* The bitter cup I so feared was becoming a reality.

The Promise of Joy

*I*n a few days the swelling diminished and her speech began to return. Two MRIs and the surgical removal of some tissue for a biopsy were conducted to tell us what we were up against. Laurie was diagnosed with a grade 3 anaplastic astrocytoma, a form of aggressive brain cancer that has no cure. We had three medical weapons with which to fight:

surgery, which due to the depth and location of the tumor was impossible for us, radiation, and chemotherapy. Yet whatever battles we chose to fight with this enemy, we would lose in the end. All that the efforts could accomplish would be to delay death and promote some quality of life. That was the best medicine could offer. I had to draw the answers out of the doctors with relentless questions. They talked to us of vague hopes, clinical studies, pills, and painkillers. In their concern for our despair their words were guarded, walking the outside boundaries rather than the center of truth.

The words stunned to a degree of numbness that looks everywhere for help, for hope, and finds none. The world was muted, like living underwater. I knew the fear of death now. What an antagonist he was. I turned to the story of Hezekiah weeping before the Lord because Isaiah had told him he was to die and to be prepared. He turned his face to the wall and asked for more life, and the Lord had Isaiah return to him and grant him fifteen more years. As an assurance to strengthen his faith, the Lord had the sundial shadow move backwards, symbolic of the rewinding of time in his behalf (see 2 Kings 20:1–11). It was the most important story in the Bible for me at that moment, and I began to ask the Lord for our own "Hezekiah time." I could not define the amount, for I felt He would be more gracious with us if we left it to his wisdom and mercy. But could He not draw the shadow on our sundial back also, if only a few degrees?

We brought Laurie home from the hospital and gathered all the family. Through the kindness of Sheri Dew, a most thoughtful friend, and Wendy Watson Nelson, who grew up in Laurie's small hometown in Alberta, Elder Russell M. Nelson came to the house and gave Laurie a blessing. He gave us needed hope to get through the next months. It was a blessing of joy—happy, radiant, lovely, redeeming joy was in her future. When he had finished, he took her hands into his and told her of his conviction that joy awaited. It was a second witness to his own inspired words.

During that blessing, I saw her running again in the visions of the mind, but not toward a stairway. She was eager, young, vital, full of life, pain-free, beautiful, and with that lightness in her step I had not seen in years. She was hurrying toward a group of people. They awaited her with gladness. Her father, who had passed away seven years previously, and her beloved Uncle Mark, who was also in the spirit world, both stepped forward to embrace her. Both sets of grandparents approached. She was loved and knew how deeply. She turned and looked back to me and her family still struggling through mortality and knew how intensely she was loved *here* and how necessary she was for our happiness, for my happiness. Her passing revealed to both her and us the quality of that love. How acutely it is felt now and continues to expand, but its deepest awareness was bought at the price of separation. Could I have possibly learned this any other way? I believe, I affirm, deeper than surface doubts, that she is now lovelier than she was on earth, but I am not there to see it, and even the remembrance of that visionary moment of joy can merely foster the thirst without quenching it. There is comfort in blessings, in the revealed ponderings and imaginations of the mind, in religion's promises, but we do not know in the manner that cries out for knowledge. Our comforts do not lie in the realm of proof, but in that of faith and love, and we must learn to be content with that.

"I SHALL CLASP THEE AGAIN"

*I*s death the enemy? Surely it brought the ache within my heart that will not, perhaps must not be abated, but that soreness of soul is becalmed by a sense of peace and gratitude. Peace that she is at peace, and gratitude that my feelings for her have been intensified. These have been days of pain, the greatest I have ever known, but also of profound love. Nothing could possibly have shown me more than Laurie's losing battle with cancer how very much I love her and will always love her. That above all else has been made crystal clear. Death, as part of that great plan of happiness and mercy, intensifies our need for each other like nothing else can. And so I am grateful for its lessons, though the cost is so immeasurably high. To love at all is to expose the soul to the possibility of pain. Only in the blackest regions of outer darkness is there no love, and that is a torment of its own kind and making. Here our grief would go, but only if the love departed also, and who would be willing to escape suffering at that price? No, rather we would bear an increase in our anguish to feel, to know beyond all misgivings, hesitations, disbeliefs, and doubts, the joy of being loved and of loving.

Many times, like most of us with those dearest to us, I have taken Laurie for granted, did not tell her enough how much she meant to me because, though I loved her and expressed that love, I did not know myself how deep the roots had grown. Now there is no doubt, no reservation—all is certainty, pure confidence. I cannot find the space within where I could say, "Here is the dwelling place she does not touch, where her absence is not missed." I know—and I hope and believe that she now knows—how completely she dominates the soul and thoughts of her husband. She fills a place within that no other being and nothing else can. Therein is our joy and our distress at separation, the paradox of God's earthly schooling, which wishes above all other considerations to teach men and women to become eternally one.

Time cannot heal or fill her absence, for time has no voice, or smile, or heart. I do not anticipate it will—only that I will grow familiar with the loss as it becomes a natural part of my life, not as debilitating and raw as it is now, but in attendance all the same. What can I place in that empty center that her presence once filled? Hours? Months? Years? The only replacement for the absence of Laurie is Laurie. Nothing can truly make up the loss of those we love, and in some sense it would be unwise to attempt to do so. Endurance is what God asks of us, and endure we must, but it need not be a distressing endurance. We hold on until reunion ends our wanting. It is not easy, but we feel the love while we wait, and love is always a good thing to fill a heart. God himself cannot replace the absence, nor do I believe He wishes to do so.

Though He would soothe the wound, complete healing is not the desired outcome. Leaving it tender preserves the seal between us, draws us ever toward each other again. All this even at the terrible price of some of our bitterest tears. Death has taught me thus. Please do not misunderstand: happiness may be found within the bonds of new relationships, but those will be formed in open places of an expanding heart, without invading the sanctity of love already lodged there.

I do not fear death anymore, though I felt its dreaded footfalls each day I woke and looked at my wife sleeping beside me. My own passing will bring reunion, which reunion is now my most sincere prayer. I do not pray for death, nor wish it to come for me early, but for the assurance of eternal oneness with Laurie. Since death is the portal to the flowering of that oneness, when it comes I will not turn from it. I once viewed it from the perspective of the plan of salvation; now it is personal.

Upon the death of his wife, poet Robert Browning's whole view of dying changed, particularly as it awaited him at some future date. It was not something he feared; rather, he welcomed it, not in anticipation, but in the culmination it would effect. He wrote the following words, which so wonderfully express how I now feel myself. They are from a poem titled "Prospice," which means "to look forward." Laurie and I had loved the ending to this poem before as we had read it together. It speaks depth of emotion to me now. I quoted it to Laurie during the last days of her life as a testimony to my own future. At that time she could not move or speak but could still listen. She was also able to still shed tears, which became at the end her only way of communicating. Her tears told me she understood.

> I was ever a fighter, so—one fight more,
> The best and the last!
> I would hate that death bandaged my eyes, and forbore,
> And bade me creep past.
> No! let me taste the whole of it, fare like my peers
> The heroes of old,
> Bear the brunt, in a minute pay glad life's arrears
> Of pain, darkness and cold.
> For sudden, the worst turns the best to the brave,
> The black minutes at end,
> And the elements' rage, the fiend voices that rave,
> Shall dwindle, shall blend,
> Shall change, shall become first a peace out of pain,
> Then a light, then thy breast,
> O thou soul of my soul! I shall clasp thee again,
> And with God be the rest.

Is it possible that death can be beautiful because so much love is born anew, refreshed in the heart like spring rain on green grass or the dew on waxed petals? If she's waiting, when I see her again, heaven will not be disappointing. It is not really "many mansions," celestial glory, or galactic splendor as some everlasting reward I desire. They will all come after with her. She is the vital link. She is all that matters. Can anything else hold eternity together?

CHAPTER IV

GOOD-BYES

... O my friend.
Men could not part us with their worldly jars,
Nor the seas change us, nor the tempests bend:
Our hands would touch for all the mountain-bars,—
And, heaven being rolled between us at the end,
We should but vow the faster for the stars.

Sonnet Two

Do Not Linger

*J*am so often surprised by the turnings of my mind. There is no road map for grief to tell us how near we are to that desired, and yet not desired, destination of healing, peace, and relief. It is desired because I cannot believe life can go on for much longer with this stone weighing down every thought. Yet would the easing of pain mean a lessening of the love, of the separation? What do I really want? That is easy to answer—I want Laurie, but at this time she is exactly what I cannot have. I talk to her constantly, and that aloud, not in my mind. I hope she is listening. How much of a conversation is allowed the marriage of the mortal living and the spirit living? I use this last description as I assume they would not consider themselves dead, but as fully alive as we are in their own sphere. I also find every prayer to God is now vocal. Those spoken in the mind seem no longer

47

sufficient. It is as if I want to part the curtain with the quality of my voice.

I tell myself every day that I must not "linger in the valley of sorrow." That is a very useful phrase, written by Nephi (2 Nephi 4:26) just after the death of his father—so he would know. That loss made him eloquent beyond anything else he had ever written, and we all love those wonderfully healing words we call the "psalm of Nephi" (see 2 Nephi 4:16-35). His grief humanized him on a scale we all can feel. It made him think on his own imperfections and weaknesses. Suffering is intimate, but it is also universal. How easily we can relate to that insight into the character of arguably the most perfect individual in the Book of Mormon. Perhaps that is part of its need in our lives.

Nephi continued his efforts to write his way out of his despondency by telling himself he could not let his "strength slacken" or his "flesh waste away" (v. 26). There is a strange idleness, a heaviness, a lethargy, a weariness about grief, a slackening and wasting. No one really depends on me anymore. I'm not responsible for anyone. If I let myself, I could do nothing day after day. What would it matter? I know that won't do, life goes on, but sometimes I look at the passing parade of people and wonder how everything can be so normal for everyone. They listen to music and don't cry? Do they not realize something profound has happened? The world has changed; something is wrong and can't be made right again. I look at couples holding hands and pause to think, "That was once mine." They look at me and think, "That may one day be one of us."

THE COLORED WORLD OF THE DANCE

Shortly before Laurie died, I dreamed I was standing by a rock wall dressed in a plain white T-shirt and a black leather jacket watching a party of very happy men and women, many of them paired in couples, dressed in vibrant party colors. They were moving away from me, going to attend some festival or dance. The mood was celebratory, holiday-like, a kind of June joy. They were all laughing. It feels like that sometimes now. I'm in a solitary, black-and-white world while the dance of life continues with its merry mirth and vivid colors. In the meantime I keep looking for a map to tell me how far I've come, where I am heading, and when I will arrive. Have I not been also invited, if I could just follow the dancers?

I tried the other day to imagine my reunion with Laurie "on the other side," as we say. I hungered for what I have often called "a pondering," one of those times when the Lord helps my imagination teach me truths. God speaks to us in our own language, which may be different for each of us, and much of mine focuses on the scenery of the mind. He did not fail me. My thoughts filled with images of a formal English ball where guests are introduced in the palace at the head of the stairs. I was not in black and white, but part of the colored world this time. Laurie was on my arm, her touch light and gentle, like it was the very first night I took her out that icy November evening. "I'll just hang on to you," she said, "then I won't fall." How I have wondered about the deeper meaning of those words and if I've lived up to them. In my "pondering," when we paused at the top of the stairs and the man who was announcing the new arrivals asked me how I would like to be presented, I said, "Tell them I'm the man Laurie Chipman loves." I never liked long introductions anyway, and I can't think of an honor that could possibly mean more to me. I just want to be the man Laurie loves. Then there will be no prolonged lingering.

THE FIRST GOOD-BYE

Color is healing. Sunshine and scenery are becoming my salvation. They were for Laurie also. It is difficult to linger in sorrow when the eyes are greeted with God's handiwork. How lifting was that November trip to southern Utah to see those red-rock panoramas. I pushed her in the wheelchair up the "Narrows" in Zion National Park and along the rims of Bryce and, finally, Kolob Canyon. We laughed at my efforts to maneuver the wheelchair over the bumps and up the sandy hills. Laurie was a notorious backseat driver, and this continued with the wheelchair. Most of what she said I could not understand, but I knew I was not steering well enough. It was another one of those endearments to be treasured.

I repeat, it is hard to stay depressed when looking at

such magnificence. I remember Anne Frank talking of how important it was for her to look out the tiny window of her hiding place and see the sky, the sunshine, and the branches of a tree. "God wishes to see people happy, amidst the simple beauty of Nature," she wrote. "As long as this exists, and it certainly always will, I know that then there will always be comfort for every sorrow, whatever the circumstances may be. And I firmly believe that nature brings solace in all troubles" (*Diary of a Young Girl*, 158). This is profound philosophy for a young girl, but then, she knew what it was to be afraid.

I must remember this and let nature work her wonder as the future's battles close in. Did not Joseph Smith teach us that God's creations were "to please the eye and to gladden the heart . . . and to enliven the soul" (Doctrine and Covenants 59:18-19)? Heart-gladdening was what both Laurie and I craved, and nature did not disappoint. There was a moment in Zion National Park when she stood at the edge of the canyon and looked across it to the massive cliffs of rose and cream, brilliant in the warm light of an evening sun. She remained wrapped in contemplation for a long time. Though I never asked her about it, I sensed she was saying her first good-bye—to this beautiful world she had hiked and explored and drawn and learned about. She had maintained a childlike sense of wonder at nature's artistry. I trust she will gaze upon even more soul-enlivening landscapes in the world to which she goes.

THE NIGHTTIME GOOD-BYES

*P*erhaps grief isn't a journey at all, but the placing of pieces in a jigsaw puzzle. We know what the picture is supposed to look like when it is complete, we have the pattern, but we wrestle with fitting it all together, and some sections are frustratingly inhospitable to our most determined efforts. Does each person have his or her own picture, and do others place their own pieces as they find they fit? Will yours look like mine so you can help me through it? Will I be able to help you? Did you have the chance to say good-bye?

We almost did not have that opportunity, and I have the greatest empathy for those whose beloved are taken suddenly and without warning. We could have lost Laurie during the initial seizures. How would I have felt if that first phone call in Atlanta had informed me my wife had died? Yet I did not have a formal "good-bye" with Laurie. We never had a real conversation that acknowledged what was happening and how she felt about it. She could not bring herself to say, "I am dying." She never wanted to look at the MRIs except once, after radiation, and that was a devastating experience because the cancer was growing when we had such expectation that it would have stabilized at least. We had imagined there was to be Hezekiah time. I try hard to forget her poignant, hopeful leaning forward from her chair as the images first came up on the computer screen, only to sink back when the doctor informed us the tumor had grown. She couldn't talk about it after that. Maybe she had a reserve of hope none of the rest of us had and continued to believe beyond belief until the cancer forbade her saying good-bye because the words or the ideas could not now form. Maybe she knew the reality of her situation and did not want to burden us with her own sorrows.

She came close one day during our last trip when we were on the Amazon River. Up to that day she had done everything on the itinerary, but she was too exhausted to take the smaller boat up a side river and climb to the canopy walk. When I returned to the room that evening she was lying on the bed. As I settled down beside her, she turned and, looking into my face, said, "I'm not staying, am I?" There were no tears, just a frightened hesitation. "No," I said, "you're going home." That was all she allowed.

There should have been a time for a final verbal exchange of love. For me it would have been so healing, so doubt suppressing. It would have silenced that dark, whispered fear inside that she may not choose to be my Laurie through eternity—that my eternal courtship had been weighed in the balance and found wanting. I was so desperate at the end to hear her say, "Michael, I love you and always will. I will wait for you." I have read and reread her notes and cards from the past and found some comfort in her expressions of affection and love. Finally, while cleaning out our closet, I found a brief autobiography under a stack of her papers, which I did not know she had written. It was dated October 2005. Midway through I read: "My favorite person is my husband . . ." It was a needed good-bye—such relief there. Had she said nothing, I would have tipped over the cliff of my fears. So I have only the sincerest empathy for those whose loved ones pass with unanticipated quickness. Thus we learn the necessity of daily expressing our hearts and of leaving reminders behind.

At the very end, when Laurie could not move or speak but could still listen and understand, I did all I could to assure her of my own love. This, I believe, is the most critical thing, more important than hearing it in return. Let not our regrets include a failure to express our hearts. She slept twenty hours at a time and awoke only for short periods, often in the earliest hours of the morning when all in the house was quiet and dark. I slept on the floor in the family room next to her bed. I waited to hear a change in her breathing or a slight motion of her head to tell me she was awake and aware. She stirred a tiny bit. I held her hand and told her, "I'd go with you, Laurie, if God would let me." I told her that she had brought me the greatest happiness of my life. I told her that she would always be in my heart, and I asked her to tell the Lord that I wanted to come as quickly as He or life would permit. I showed her the pictures I had specially framed so I could take her with me wherever I traveled. It was the only way we could in some measure continue with our dreams. She could not squeeze my hand in acknowledgment, but she could cry, and I saw the tears come and felt I had an answer. Three times I shared these same words, on three separate nights, and three times she responded with her tears. At the very end, even tears were denied her.

Good-byes are so essential, so significant. Perhaps that is the real reason why I write. Though no one else may read my words, I believe she will, and that will be enough. Are we not told that some things are recorded in heaven as they are on earth? I was not blessed with twenty years in the gracefulness of life with her, but I can give her my thoughts, a written inheritance, and that may be worth some of those missed years to her.

"For Her!"

*O*ne would think that the memory of those nighttime tears would be enough—as surely they must be, I keep affirming to myself—yet this morning, even after having written of our farewells in the night, even after the discovery of her life's story, I was gripped with the familiar doubts. All the black miseries of grief, the nightmare fears that burden and tighten the chest, returned in one engulfing wave, and I could not pray nor weep my way out of them. Our bereavements seem to have no prophets to circumscribe their limits or foretell the paths they may take. Perhaps grief is not a journey with signposts to tell us we are nearing the end. It is more like a fog that lifts and descends, giving us clear and hopeful views and then obscuring the path again. Yet I must believe that there will come a gradual lifting—filtered and muted sunlight widening to warming rays. There is often no reasoning in my dark moments, just pure emotion. I am beginning to understand poor Thomas now and his need to see and touch in spite of every other witness. "Blessed are they that have not seen," Jesus told him, "and yet have believed" (John 20:29). That blessedness may have more to do with the torments of fears and doubts on the man himself than some form of righteousness attributed to those whose faith does not demand the tangible. They are simply happier in their need not to know as Thomas needed to know.

Regardless, the cold fear and sorrow returns like ice in my heart that, temporarily at least, no warmth of memory, hope, or eternal covenant can melt. But my course is never doubted, and I tell myself, sometimes hourly, that I must be the noblest, kindest, most forgiving and Godlike man I can be, so that when we meet after the twilight of my own life, I can say, "Look, Laurie, what I've become! Look what longing for you has wrought! Look how the separation has changed me! I wasn't in mortality all that you deserved, all that would make you happy, but I am much closer now!"

Why is it so easy to idealize Laurie's every virtue and to dismiss, without a breath of a thought, her every weakness—to see only loveliness, grace, sacrifice, and perfected refining femininity in her and only folly, insensitivity, and weakness in myself? Is this the last great motivator, death's spur that pricks us on to perfection? I yearn for Godliness for her sake, perhaps more than for God's eternal purposes. But then, that is to the fulfilling of His purposes. Jesus so strongly taught, "Wherefore they are no more twain, but one," and that for time and all eternity (Matthew 19:6).

I remember reading of a moment shared by a fellow sailor of Sir Ernest Shackleton, the great Antarctic explorer, who told of the impact Emily Dorman, Shackleton's wife, had on her husband. The two mariners were standing on the deck of a ship when the conversation took place.

"'Well, Shacky,' I remarked one evening, 'and what do you think of this old tub? You'll be skipper of her one day.' 'You see, old man,' he said, 'as long as I remain with this company I'll never be more than a skipper. But I think I can do something better. In fact, really, I would like to make a name for myself'—he paused for a moment or two—'and for her.' He was looking pensively over the sea at the moment, and I noticed his face light up at the mention of 'her.' In my bunk that night I felt convinced that the ambition of that man's life was to do something worthy—not only for himself, but 'for her'" (Riffenburgh, *Shackleton's Forgotten Expedition*, chapter 3). My course is perfection for her as well as for Him, doing something good every day, with love of both being the main motivation.

THE UNEXPECTED GOOD-BYE

*L*aurie had the opportunity to see all those most close to her during the last few days of her life. Though unspoken, good-byes were exchanged as best they could be. The last full night of her life, her breathing had already become irregular, and I thought several times, "This will be the last breath." Yet even after a pause of three or four of my own breaths, she would inhale deeply, hold the air, and then let it out slowly before continuing rhythmically for a short time. This pattern was repeated throughout the night.

About three in the morning, she stirred the tiniest bit. I rose, took her hand, and told her it was time to go home and she could go in peace. There was no need to hold on to life anymore. All had been achieved that needed to be. She had been an adored wife, devoted mother and grandmother, loving daughter, sincere friend. Glory awaited her. It was all right to let go. But there was one last good-bye, and it took place as I sat silently by her side feeling the profound reverence of the moment. It was so unexpected, and yet so obviously necessary, I wondered that I had never thought of it before. It was her spirit bestowing upon her body its gratitude and love. She was saying good-bye to a part of herself, the mortal, physical part that had brought such blessings to her.

It seemed I was listening to a sacred conversation between two separate beings, yet they were one and the same. The body was not like a warm coat in winter to house the spirit, but something, almost *someone*, to share life with, to love and enjoy—an approaching-equal entity of independent yet dependent, reliant life. I was not part of that farewell, but felt so very thankful that I was not dismissed as it took place. The love between body and spirit was as strong as that between man and woman, between mother and child. It was deep and abiding, with a longing in it that went beyond the most endearing friendship but contained elements of that bond within it. It was holy, a sacrament of some type I could barely comprehend.

Though the physical part of her was dying and had given her prolonged pain, how she loved that body. It had borne her children. Its feminine beauty had drawn her husband to her. Through these eyes she had viewed the wonders of the world. These ears had resonated with the melody of song. Through the skill of her hands and voice she had found fulfillment in the refinement of art and music. Her body had brought delight, sensation, touch, taste, and smell, enabling her to enjoy all the pleasures of mortality. It had taught her discipline, strengthening her will and ennobling her spirit. Now they were parting, and there was sadness mingled with the gratitude, but above all enduring love.

This was enhanced by the knowledge that of all the reunitings that would take place in the future—daughter to parent, wife to husband, mother to child—that of spirit to body would have the longest wait. All the others could take place in the world of spirits, but this reunion must hold till the resurrection. Here, too, dying was teaching me profound lessons about love. I now believe I understand why element and spirit, "united never again to be divided," create the fulness of joy, and why the resurrection of Christ is such a supreme gift (Doctrine and Covenants 138:17). It is the culmination and eternal fulfillment of uniting love, similar to, though distinct from, the desire I have never to be divided from her again.

MOUNT NEBO: THE DISTANT GOOD-BYE

I stood on Mount Nebo in Jordan a few months after her death. On a clear day you can just make out the towers on the top of the Mount of Olives overlooking Jerusalem far in the distance. Here Moses, after a long and enriching life of service to God, was shown the land he would not visit, would not walk upon. "Get thee up into this mountain . . . and die in the mount whither thou goest up, and be gathered unto thy people" (Deuteronomy 32:49–50). He was 120 years old and yet still grieved when life was over for its being over so soon. He had to say good-bye to his dream. "O Lord God," he prayed, "thou hast begun to shew thy servant thy greatness, and thy mighty hand. . . . I pray thee, let me go over, and see the good land that is beyond Jordan, that goodly mountain" (Deuteronomy 3:24–25). What an interesting word is Moses' *begun*, given as it was at the ending. I understand his heart. Laurie too wanted to see "that goodly mountain." It was a tough good-bye. I thought of all the times I had stood in this identical spot with her, never realizing she would climb her own Mount Nebo gazing at an anticipated future life she would not live, not knowing yet the coming life God would grant her in the world to which she traveled. She would have to say good-bye to the looked-for life, the expected and desired life, to let it go.

How many have shared with Moses the prayer of yearning? God answered Moses, and us in him, with four simple words, "Let it suffice thee . . ." (Deuteronomy 3:26). I must accept this answer also, as Laurie had to, and as must so many others who know what it is to stand on the mountaintop and look longingly into the distance at a denied destination. But I suppose no duration of life is sufficient for all the hopes, and dreams, and good of which it is capable. Ultimately we all share this good-bye.

UNSPOKEN

*H*ow do you say good-bye to the woman you love, the friend who is more than friend? How do you say good-bye to a part of yourself? I haven't learned this yet. I could tell her with such peace that it was all right for her to go, but I could not say the word to her then, nor will it come now, even in the silence of my own mind. I feel it inside of me pushing up sometimes, but I weigh it down and smother it. I must not allow it to rise to the level of a spoken word or even an acknowledged thought. If it escapes it will crush me. It is the one thing that I cannot do, nor do I think I will ever be able to do it. I believe I can bear her loss as long as I don't have to say good-bye. It is a wall too high for me to climb over. The finality of it is too overwhelming. I don't know if others feel this or not. Maybe that is why she couldn't say it either. Could it be that this is an unconscious witness that we don't need to say it because there is no such finality? Yet, it is possible that she needs that release to move forward into her own new world in greater tranquility. A friend suggested that to me, but I keep hoping I'll always feel her approach and there will be no need for my own good-bye.

"Forgive me, Laurie, I cannot do it. I can let you go, but not that far."

I cannot continue to write about it, even in my own private notes, for it creates despair rather than releasing it. It will remain unspoken.

CHAPTER V

LOOKING ACROSS, LOOKING AWAY

How do I love thee? Let me count the ways.
I love thee to the depth and breadth and height
My soul can reach, when feeling out of sight
For the ends of Being and ideal Grace.

Sonnet Forty-Three

FAR BETTER OR MORE NEEDFUL

*S*ome measure of healing came one morning about two weeks after her death. I've become somewhat euphemistic about that word. I guess we all prefer "her passing." Insight comes slowly, and it seems as if the days are twice as long as before, but it does come. I was in the Antarctic going over old notes and rereading passages from books about the explorers of this "last place on earth." I had been thinking too much, which only succeeded in making the days more difficult. It has always been my way to reason, to philosophize, to mull things over, or to talk my way out of a problem. Keep mentally circling, and eventually an opening will come that will penetrate to the heart of the matter and end the constant turning. I search for some scripture, some crafted piece of prose, or rhyme of poetry, or cogent argument that will close the wound. Laurie was content to let things rest for a while, to hope life would solve itself. I keep trying to find some thought, some logical conclusion, some discourse or debate I can have with myself that will make suffering cease to be suffering, but the smallest memory can bring my best efforts crashing down.

The final stage of Laurie's cancer went so quickly. During the months of our battle there were many times when I did not know what to pray for. "My own vision is so limited," I finally told the Lord, "that I know not what is best. Please choose for us the proper path to the right outcome. Do not be indifferent to our desires. We trust Thy wisdom and mercy. The issues of life and death are so great and our own experience and thoughts so insufficient, how can we know what is right? What shall I ask for?"

I thought so often, during those months, of Paul's words to his beloved Philippians when he was awaiting his trial in Rome. "For to me to live is Christ, and to die is *gain*. But if I live in the flesh, this is the fruit of my labour: yet what I shall choose I wot not. For I am in a strait betwixt two, having a desire to depart, and to be with Christ; which is *far better*: Nevertheless to abide in the flesh is *more needful* for you" (Philippians 1:21-24, emphasis added).

Those two phrases, "far better" and "more needful," lift from the page. With Laurie were we in a "far better" or a "more needful" position? Could we even accept the "far better" equation? I used to come up with all the "more needfuls" I could, but none of them were strong enough to outweigh the "far better" I anticipated the Lord would lean toward. So I had to pray, "Thy will be done," not as an act of obedience but as one of trust because I had not sufficient knowledge to have a will of my own that I could present to Him with any confidence. If it were far better for her to be with Him, how could I pray that it would be otherwise?

I remembered Paul also teaching the Romans that the Spirit sometimes intercedes for us when we know not what to pray (see Romans 8:26). Therefore, I often asked, "What shall I pray for?" And, in time, He answered, "Pray that she might drain all the joy out of the cup of mortality and then pass quickly to her rest." That became my prayer.

On the first of December we invited hospice in to take over all medical issues. They would be easier to work with in obtaining what we needed. The doctors had done the best they could, and we had no more interest in trying new treatments with hollow hopes. It was time to turn to the sunset. The hospice nurse told us on December 4 that if Laurie continued to have her strength, there was every possibility that we could go south in January. I wanted her to have the joy of returning to Antarctica with me because we had so enjoyed our earlier trip the year before; we shared such a love of the explorers, wildlife, and scenery of that region of the world.

But the cancer continued to grow. Four days later, when the nurse came in next, Laurie had begun the final rapid decline that ended her life in barely three weeks, on December 28.

It is difficult to see someone who was so vital, so full of life and energy, lose every function one by one. She lost the ability to speak, to walk, then the movement of her right leg, then the right arm. Next came the stilling of the left leg and then the left arm. The last few days she could not move her head. Finally, the day she died, even her eyelids would not flutter, and the tears that I so counted on ceased. Three short weeks. But she could hear the joys of Christmas as her loved ones gathered on Christmas Eve in the family room where we had placed her bed. On the night of the twenty-seventh she began to breathe very rapidly and heavily, the way one would after having run a great distance. I listened to her for hours, thinking again what a wonderful thing it was to draw another breath. I repeat, how precious is life, such a great gift with so much of the divine in it. Only breath and the beating of her heart were left to her now.

I stayed by her side, fearful of leaving the room, and four of our children came over to the house. Her breathing suddenly slowed about one in the morning. She took five tiny, peaceful breaths hardly above a whisper and that was all. It was a calm, solemn moment; even weeping seemed inappropriate for the level of reverence we all felt. I was not shattered until the mortuary came to take her from the house and the sight of her leaving undid me. *Far better* does not always mean *far easier*.

LOOKING AWAY AS WELL AS ACROSS

I needed to stay active. I could not sit in the house. Each night, I planned the next day before going to sleep so I would know exactly what I was going to do. My daughters tried to keep me company constantly until my departure on the sixth of January for Antarctica. I was grateful for the distraction, for somewhere to go, and for friends to be with. As I turned the pages of books Laurie and I had both read on Antarctica I could see her underlining and notes everywhere. How we both loved this region! I read a new book about Shackleton on the flight to South America, and the first note I wrote myself was, "How Laurie would have loved this book!" There was not sadness, though, in the thought, but a kind of peace and enjoyment that was doubled because the woman I loved would have loved it too. It was a comfortable feeling, common ground, like going home. I had prepared a talk the previous trip on the splendors of creation. The last point I had recorded in my notes simply stated, "And I get to share all this with Laurie."

There is a love that is developed between two people who look across at each other and love what they see. It is found in the face and features, in the heart, and hair, and soul, and mind each accepts as a gift from the other. But all this is enhanced by the love that unites when both look from each other to something else and each loves what the eyes see equally. Our marriage was more than just us. It was everything we both found dear, or satisfying, or comic, or lovable. It was the Shakespeare Festival, and Chinese art, the sea cliffs of Ireland, the Canadian Rockies, and the red rock hiking trails of southern Utah. It was BBC miniseries and Poirot mysteries, orange juice with popcorn, the lyrics of a dozen different songs, and French toast in the morning.

I sat alone at a table in the dining room on the cruise ship looking at the empty chair across from me. I wanted so much to see her sitting there as she had the year before. I tried to visualize her form and imagine what she would say to me. But she was not there, and my imagination, usually so reliable, failed me. Yet when I turned and looked at the white wilderness and blue icebergs of Antarctica that we had shared and loved together, I felt her draw near. It was not a presence, not a voice, but a warm flowing over the soul, a quiet awareness of someone looking with me and loving what I saw. It was akin to trying to retrieve an early morning dream or a forgotten lyric, that snatch of song that trembles just on the rim of the mind. If I turned to see her, there was only the empty chair, but when I looked away I felt that otherness sharing with me again. She was a part of me in that which we both loved, in things I could still see and smell and taste and feel.

Maybe she went a bit more quickly in December so I could come to that unique part of the world where we had shared our last pre-cancer time together with such delight, such anticipation of the coming retired life, where she gave that inspiring talk on Shackleton that was better than any I gave throughout the tour. Here I could learn that in those things we both loved I would sometimes sense her near, not in a nostalgic turning to the past with its cherished memories, but in feeling the ties continue to bind through beloved things and places and people. I sensed this would be true in all things from the simplest note she penned in the margins of a book to the grandest majesty of scenic beauty. I receive at times the same quiet gentleness, the sharing, when I see my children and grandchildren. I anticipate it may come with every tiny piece of life that I knew we both loved or would have come to love had she remained.

I still look for her across the table, and the empty chair always gives me pain, but there is an easing of the ache when I look away in the distance. There is something near that I must take into account. Enoch described God as being "there" when talking of the grand immensity of God's creations and of His love (Moses 7:30). Laurie is simply "there."

As I see and learn new things, I will continue to say, "Laurie would have loved this!" That is a type of sharing I can still have with her. And perhaps, somewhere next to a heavenly landscape, she too stands and says, "Mike would love this!" I expect, I hope, she is making her own list of things and people and vistas that she will share with me when we are reunited and can look across at each other again as well as away to what she has discovered and found beautiful, but could not totally enjoy until we gazed on it together.

ONLY ONE-THIRD LEFT

*A*nd there will be those times when the presence becomes more than the shadow of herself. I am grateful for the shadows, the echoes, the reflections, the oh-so-near mirages, but I need something more real, more substantial, something I won't always question as the result of my own need to believe she is really near. Then I believe it will be allowed, if permission is even necessary, for her to come again and to linger without any sense of the need to depart until we are comforted. We speak of missionary work and the hurry, excitement, joy, and occupation of the spirit world, but she is still my wife. More than missionary is mother. If we need her, we need her, and she will fulfill her most eternal roles to the fullest extent of allowed possibility as the veil thins.

On a particularly difficult morning I was feeling so incomplete, feeling like frayed cloth, torn and unraveling, with the threads hanging loose, diminished, feeling I was only one-third of what I used to be. There was Laurie—the "her." There was Michael—the "I." And there was Michael and Laurie—the "us." Two of those were gone. I picked up one of her favorite books, opened the front cover, and saw written in her hand, "S. Michael and Laura Wilcox." There was a tug of pain, then calm, and I smiled. The letters, written in that graceful, feminine script with which I was so familiar—because for years she had copied in pen the penciled notes I had written in my scriptures so they would look neat and clean—seemed to say, "See! We're still together. Our names are not parted. There is still 'us'!"

Preparing a Place

There must be more to the spirit world than just missionary work. Teaching, of course, but learning, too.

Certainly there will be new tutorials, knowledge gathered—and at a much accelerated pace. She will acquire the skills of creation, from the coloring of a bird's feather to the songs of the wind. What wonders will she be able to teach me when I arrive? Would she not also be engaged in the preparation of an eternal home, whatever that might mean? "Mike will want both a Chinese and an English garden," she would conclude. Yet that may be reasoning limited by earth's frontiers, beauty and order barely comparable to paradisiacal possibilities. With what delight would she say, "Come, let me show you what I've been doing!" How she loved decorating every corner of the house each December for the family to enjoy. Of course, I don't know, but Jesus told those he loved, his friends, "Let not your heart be troubled. . . . In my Father's house are many mansions. . . . I go to prepare a place for you. And if I go and prepare a place for you, I will come again, and receive you unto myself; that where I am, there ye may be also" (John 14:1–3).

We ardently desire this union with Christ, but do not the words also vividly express the depth of feeling we have for each other? How beautiful they are to read with this in mind. Will she partner herself with our Savior in preparing our tiny corner, our "place," in the grand order of continuing creation? The feeling of "us" becomes stronger and pushes back the idea that I am only a third of what I once was, torn apart and continuing to fray. As I read the words of Jesus, I feel him allowing Laurie to share them with Him. I can almost hear her saying to me: "I go to prepare a place for us.

Soon, I will come again and receive you unto myself. Where I am, there you will be also." Excitedly she would show me all that she had accomplished and learned, and the home she had been preparing. Teaching! Learning! Preparing! How could I be anything but joyful for her? My great-grandfather left his wife in Denmark while he came to America early to prepare a home for them. When all was arranged, he sent for her and showed her all he had completed for their mutual happiness. Perhaps it's like that.

"I Feel No Guilt"

There is a great capacity for joy in the human soul that no earthly thing can fill, but loving and being loved by another comes close. It changes one. I believed this before. I have death's witness of it now. Its unquestioned confirmation has come at the price of parting and suffering. I remember Mark Twain writing about his love for his own wife through the character of Adam standing at Eve's grave with the wonderfully simple and unadorned truth, "Wheresoever she was, there was Eden." There was a time, very early in her trials, when the freshness of Eden rested upon Laurie, and I was changed once again by my love for her.

The first days, blending even into the first two weeks after the seizures had brought Laurie so close to death, left her with a certain light, a refining elegance. There was a translucent quality about her, very difficult to articulate, but received by those who were around her. The soul shining through the physical more intensely is the only way I can describe it. There had been a cleansing of some sort through her brushing so close to the veil, a new initiatory. This was one of the great compensatory gifts that accompanied those first nightmare days of cancer's realities. She said more than once that for the first time in her remembered life she could feel no guilt, no shame, no regret, and no inadequacies. She was at total peace with herself. This brought for me a rare touch of joy, for she was a normal Mormon woman who never felt she fully measured up and struggled with self-acceptance in her demanding world and life with me. Yet, God never made a better woman.

Why do we see our insufficiencies so clearly and in such a way as to dim even the brightest lights of our goodness? But those first days were remarkable. More than one of our friends who knew her so well commented that she seemed like an angel. They all used the same word, and I, who had lived with her and knew her more intimately than any other human being, felt the same. How this increased my affections and feelings for her and my own happiness in the midst of our fears for the future! I noticed it on the first morning she awoke after that horrible, dark night when all she could do to greet me as I walked into the ICU was to smile faintly. Now, as the swelling in her brain diminished, she was talking again, although tentatively, but the tranquility of her voice and features were decidedly different. We both felt that her father and beloved Uncle Mark had been with her during her ordeal alone before my daughter had found her on the floor tangled in the bedsheets. Had they shared something with her that took away the accumulated guilt of the past, the general unease with which we are all so familiar, and left that lucent, purifying shadow of light? Was it the echoing of things to come?

THROUGH THE FLOWER'S OPENING

*E*very religion has different symbols or metaphorical language for the dividing line between the world of the spirit and the world of the flesh, between the eternal and the temporal spheres. We use a veil or a door. The ancient Mayans sometimes referred to it with the image of a flower. It is the most helpful of all portal symbolism to describe those days with Laurie and how they affected each of us. In Mayan belief, one traveled through the flower's blossom to reach the other side, and they came into our world through the same colored passageway. The flower's scent was the air of the other existence escaping into our own through the opening of the petals. This is lovely theology! It is a description I prefer even above Christianity's waving folds of a curtained partition.

During those days the flower was opened wide behind my wife and the breezes of eternity were passing through and over her. Laurie seemed to stand in the mouth of the flower, and the fragrance of the spirit world enveloped her in its holiness. It mildly, gently, sweetly brushed away all life's accumulated negatives. It was a perfumed sacrament. We could smell heaven in her hair, see God's coloring in her eyes. How lovely she was! How calm! If loving and being loved by another is the closest thing to heavenly joy we can experience on earth, then this was a tiny foretaste of what lay at the back of the flower's center throughout eternal time. How simply and beautifully the purification had begun.

All of the children came the weekend we brought her home from the hospital. The following Thursday she had a biopsy that would once again hurl her into a world of agonizing pain and confusion, but for a few days all was peaceful, all was quiet affection. We had one of our children's friends come over to take family pictures. Laurie was the center of them all, whether with myself, our children, or our grandchildren. When the finished shots were later brought to the family, I was amazed that one could see that indefinable quality about her even in a photograph. I have pictures of Laurie when she was young; when I look at those, I think of the adjectives *pretty* or *cute*. I have those of her as my bride when she was calmly and joyfully radiant, the girl become a woman because she was loved and chosen by one man above all the women in the world. I have those when she is a mother wherein I would describe her as softly beautiful, or lovely, the giver of new life. But during that time she acquired something heavenly. As I hold the pictures in my hand, the only word that seems sufficient is *hallowed*.

I know doctrinally we speak of being the same person in the hereafter as we are here, that we take our failings and character flaws with us. I wonder. Many of them are tied so strongly to mortality, surely much of their hold unravels and there is release. Regardless, I witnessed a transformation, an initiation of sorts, the baptism of dying or coming so close to death that much of the world vanishes, leaving an innocence of spirit. This was an invitation to enter holy ground, the putting off of the dusty shoes before the burning bush of a purer world. Brigham Young once taught a delightfully pleasing and deeply comforting lesson. Though it has reference to the resurrected state, its reach encompasses what I was learning as I looked upon my wife.

"Those who attain to the blessing of the first or celestial resurrection will be pure and holy, and perfect in body. Every man and woman that reaches to this unspeakable attainment will be as beautiful as the angels that surround the throne of God. If you can, by faithfulness in this life, obtain the right to come up in the morning of the resurrection, you need entertain no fears that the wife will be dissatisfied with her husband, or the husband with the wife" (in *Journal of Discourses*, 10:24).

I suppose a major portion of that beauty has to do with the falling away of mortal cares and the offenses we do to ourselves, to others, and to our God. Is that not what Brigham Young is suggesting? And it seems to begin at the portal we call death. We are drawn through the flower with its fragrance clinging to us while the smell of the earthly dissipates.

CHAPTER VI

THE MIDNIGHT THOUGHTS

Because thou hast the faith and love to see
Through that same soul's distracting lethargy
The patient angel waiting for a place
In the new heavens . . .

Sonnet Thirty-Nine

THE UNRAVELING

*T*hose faith-filled first days may have been a gift from God, a manifestation of His love because He knew what dark nights would follow. Sometimes I would get through the day only to have my hard-won peace called to the ramparts again with the setting of the sun. I learned to dread the midnight thoughts that assailed after the closing of the day when I was alone with my own negatives. Why did such imaginings trouble me? Was I not strong in belief? I had taught the gospel for forty years. I had never really questioned the reality of eternity until I knew Laurie was going into it, knew she was going to die. I had faith, a strong testimony—how could I even entertain the uncertainty, the fear that there might be nothing after this life? "Will I ever see her again?" chased all my hopes around the racetrack of my brain. Did she go into some galactic void, into nothingness where the personality, the mind, and all the qualities of soul of what was once Laurie Wilcox ceased to exist? The heavens of the nighttime sky, which once held a wonder of mystery and invitation, were now a vast unknown, a friendless and empty place. The lone and dreary world was not here, but there.

I continued to remind myself of an earlier experience when I knew, or I thought I knew. I had perceived a dear friend happily occupied in the spirit world after an automobile accident. I had not asked for that tiny vision of the mind, nor was my faith in doubt about the doctrines of the scriptures. Why should it come then and not now, when all my happiness was weighing in the balance? I would give anything God asked to have that confirming, consoling, and doubt-breaking affirmation now, to return to the days without wondering. The great, firm knot of all my witnesses, formed in the rope of my faith by years of believing, which had seemed so securely in my grasp before, was now unraveling, leaving me only a thin line to cling to, requiring greater labor to grip it tightly, and if I fell . . .

I could never complete that thought. I ran from it.

In time I learned to minimize these demons with pure reason aside from faith. It seemed a more sturdy platform to stand upon in my reach for comfort. What would be the purpose of anything if life, if relationships did not continue? The whole of creation with all its lovely order could not end in a void. What waste that would be! To spend years nurturing love, forgiving, compromising, enduring, delighting, sharing, shaping, and carving the character, to end at the grave?—to go into nothingness? No! Eternity was certain! Abiding love was undeniable! A higher purpose than merely an earthly existence that left continuing life only in another's memory was evident! How could it be any other way and be consistent with all I saw around me?

Another fear began to surface. Laurie had tied her eternal hopes with mine. Would it not take the combined length of both faiths woven together to swing us high enough to reach heaven's door? What if my own rope was not long enough? Her eternal happiness was linked to me, a flawed man. She once wrote: "My hero" in a note addressed to me. What if I failed her, failed us, in the remaining years of my own mortality? God would see to her happiness, of course, but that stirred other fears.

IRRATIONAL FEARS—BUT FEARS

Sometimes they seemed so inconsequential, almost silly, easily discarded, but fragments clung to my mind like annoying burrs. She was young again, more beautiful than I could ever remember her; how could she continue to want an aging man? After the cancer I could never see her as anything but the girl I married thirty-eight years ago. True, I would be young also when we met again, but would her love have waned in the intervening years? How could I continue to court her and hold her heart when she was not here? Was time different, so that what seemed so long for me would be short for her? I had so planned on years of freer time with her to anchor our eternal commitment.

If that anxiety could be let go as the mortal frailty of one who thought in terms of clocks and calendars, the qualities of our souls could not. She was in a perfected state, untroubled by sin, folly, or weakness. I had seen the springtime angel rising even from the winter of her waning mortal life. During her life she was so much better than I was already. I still battled so many inheritances of the forbidden fruit—falling and failing so easily. In the spirit world one progressed more rapidly; how much farther would she be on the road to perfection? In addition, how could I hope to measure up in righteous manhood to that vast array of magnificent souls laboring in the world of spirits? My own feeble goodness would diminish against those lions of nobility, Christ himself being among them.

I was ashamed that such questions should even have a chance to disturb my peace, but fears are not rational, they are simply fears and we must deal with them in the shapes they assume until we can eliminate all that is false in our desire for truth. So often I pray:

"Please, Father, let there be my Laurie somewhere, and let her still be 'my' Laurie."

Perhaps only those who have lost one upon whom all our happiness rests will understand such challenges to faith or the calm that soothes as they are faced and driven back. To those who said to me, "You have nothing to worry about," I thought, "You simply cannot comprehend." Yet, I often say, "Why do I torment myself with such fears?"

I know God understands the nighttime thoughts, and once He reminded me of the nature of His daughters' vision. I thought of those hopeful female eyes that look to the men they love with such forgiveness and understanding, believing they will one day be all they desire them to be, believing they will in time see Christ's countenance in their own beloved's face. Part of eternal love's warmth, its sealing power, its time-erasing stretch, especially as reflected in women, is seeing and loving the becoming man even more than the existing one.

"Father, let Laurie see that man in me!"

There are times when rational argument, logic, scriptural or prophetic utterances, even prayer can't soothe the mind. It is going to despair, may create its own barriers to the Spirit, and then only love can arrest the descent. There was one very painful moment when the family was gathered around Laurie's bed in the hospital. We had just been told that the second confirming MRI indicated a form of aggressive cancer. One of the doctors told me privately that at best we could hope for two years of life if she responded to treatment; otherwise she would live only six months. They wanted to do a biopsy, which had its own dangers. I was terrified as well as on the point of total despair and broke down. Laurie could not move from the bed to respond to me, but was distressed at my crying and called out to my children, "Oh! Somebody give Dad a hug!" It was the right and only suitable response and stopped me from tumbling over the edge.

Laurie had her fears also. Most of them were not communicated. They were too difficult to meet head-on. There was a bit of Scarlett O'Hara in Laurie: "I'll worry about that tomorrow." When it was explained that there was no cure for the cancer, just the hope that death could be postponed, she alluded more than once to one of her own uncertainties. Often it came in hints, since she wasn't sure what I was thinking and the very fact that she was troubled had its own level of distress for me. We had sacrificed and saved for years to be free of debt and enjoy an early retirement without financial worries. Many of those years put a difficult strain on Laurie, yet if something happened to me I wanted her to be secure. She often teased me. "I'll do all this struggling and saving, we'll reach our goals and I'll die young. Then you'll remarry and some other woman will get all the fun." I'd answer, "You're going to live to an old age. At any rate, nobody could put up with me but you, Laurie. Besides, I'm a one-woman man!" This was a kind of romantic bantering, but underneath was a legitimate fear and a responding commitment.

Once at the beginning, while she was still in the hospital and the swelling in her brain had created a guileless openness about her, she said, "I should have been a better wife. You'll meet another woman, someone better than me, and you'll marry her." There was a plaintive, tiny little cry in her words that broke my heart. "No," I answered. "There could never be anyone but you. God never made a lovelier woman. You have brought me so much happiness. You are locked within every cell of my being. No one will replace you. I will love you always. You're the only woman I want." She reached up and touched my cheek, then let her hand drop back to the bed and looked out the window. After a while she stopped referring to it as other concerns became more urgent, but I don't think the anxiety ever left her.

"AFAR WE SEE THE GOLDEN REST"

*I*n spite of all the doctrines and comforts of the gospel, the land beyond the veil is still largely unknown country, and she would go into it alone. "Whatever happens will be for the best. There are no bad endings," I told her after we had received a negative MRI report. "God cannot ignore so many petitions by so many people that are offered so purely. Everybody loves you. Maybe all the medical doors have to close so if we get our Hezekiah time we will know it is a gift from God and nobody else." I tried hard to believe my own words. I think she saw through me, but there was a possibility in the thought, and I clung to it.

As she declined so rapidly during the last three weeks, I began to feel her father and uncle approaching. I sensed that those in the spirit world don't know exactly when their loved ones will be coming, just as we don't know when they will pass, but wait nearby so the person will not go into the unknown without one there to ease the passage. They understand more than we do the sweetness of life, even life with pain, and how hard it is to lose it. There must be something uniquely precious and wonderful about life that we are so reluctant to leave it or to watch so sorrowfully someone end it. There is more to this than just the loss of future companionship or the pain that sometimes accompanies dying. The thing itself has a sad solemnity about it, and this even when we believe we are going into a world of joy and peace to be greeted by all those we love. Leonardo da Vinci wrote: "Whatever it is, the soul is a divine thing . . . it takes its leave of the body very unwillingly, and indeed I believe that its grief and pain are not without cause" (from an anatomical folio, c. 1510, in Nicholl, *Leonardo da Vinci*, 499).

Laurie had told me earlier in her life that the one hymn she wanted sung at her funeral, if she passed before I did, was the last two verses of "The Iron Rod" (*Hymns*, no. 274):

> And, hand o'er hand, the rod along,
> Through each succeeding day,
> With earnest prayer and hopeful song,
> We'll still pursue our way.
>
> Afar we see the golden rest
> To which the rod will guide,
> Where, with the angels bright and blest,
> Forever we'll abide.

She also loved the last words of "Lead, Kindly Light" (*Hymns*, no. 97), which similarly teach of pleasing companionship in the world into which we go:

> *And with the morn those angel faces smile,*
> *Which I have loved long since, and lost awhile!*

Departed members of Laurie's family were evidently nearby on the other side of the veil, but I did not sense an excitement among them for her to come into their presence—rather, a reverent waiting and, yes, reluctance that life was ending for her. They were there to ease the loss, not to congratulate her on some sort of advancement. The reunions would be joyful, but she was leaving so much behind.

I wanted to be holding her hand as she died and dared not go out of the room in case I would miss it. I pictured her pulling away from my hand as her father took the other one to bring her into the next world. There was peace in the thought of a seamless transition of warmth. The last communication I enjoyed with her was simply the warmth of her hand, which did not diminish until she had drawn her last breath.

There is a wonderfully consoling phrase the Old Testament uses in describing the passing of the great patriarchs. It reflects the understanding of the ancients. After Jacob "yielded up the ghost," he "was gathered unto his people" (Genesis 49:33). That lovely verb, *gathered*, was used of Isaac as well (see Genesis 35:29). There is a sense of harvesting implied as well as reunion, with the whole phrase tinted with family on a large scale. It has a celebratory feel to it. Joseph said, "I die, and go unto my fathers; and I go down to my grave with joy" (JST, Genesis 50:24). Of course, he was an old man when he said this, and Laurie was only fifty-seven, with so much life left to enjoy. Yet the idea of joining with one's people as ringing with compensatory gladness is there. Shakespeare wrote, "Men must endure their going hence, even as their coming hither; ripeness is all" (*King Lear*, act IV, scene II). And Laurie was surely in full blossom.

Though we grasp this instinctively, it is so very difficult to watch the fruit leave the tree, even knowing joy will soon be coming.

"I Should Haves" and Hopes

One must also learn to deal with the regrets that nighttime grief pushes back up into the memory. These are the tiny poison darts of quick pain that continue to smart because you can't do anything now to make up for them and because the possibilities seem so countless. If you deal with one, there is always another in the queue to take its place. I sometimes feel like a man beset by hornets: I can't evade them all, and sooner or later some are going to sting. "I should have told her. . . . I ought to have done. . . . I could have been more. . . . Why did I not . . . ? Why did I . . . ? How could I have . . . ? What was I thinking . . . ? I always intended . . . I wanted to . . . I was planning on . . . We needed more time so . . . Did I tell her enough that I loved her?" They are always buzzing around my head. They are mostly little things—no single one very significant. It is the accumulation of regrets, their never-ending litany, that can bend hope downward and make the nights so much longer.

There was the rising and falling of our hopes brought on by both medical professionals and the expectations of faith and prayer. At times faith can be the cruelest hope of all because it is so entwined with what we perceive may be within our power. We question and blame ourselves for not having more. If we only had sufficient faith, would we not receive the miracle? But there is also that plaintive cry, "Lord, I believe; help thou mine unbelief" (Mark 9:24).

We dealt almost daily with offered cures from every quarter imaginable and covering a wide latitude of solutions from shark cartilage to snake venom. There were miracle workers in Italy, in Mexico, in China, at a dozen different clinics across America. I spent hundreds of hours on the Internet researching every possibility that had some merit in it, while expectations and optimism rose and fell until exhaustion set in. We simply could not try them all, nor could we continually live in hope's mirages forever. There had to come an accepting time. It arrived earlier for me than for her. Yet I often thought, "What if one of them really *would* work, and I failed Laurie because of my skepticism, fatigue, or lack of knowledge?"

Medically, we had pinned every hope on radiation when her tumor was too deep for surgery. Surely this would stop the cancer at least for a short period. I read and reread the story of Hezekiah and his pleading for more time. A loving God granted it to him! And we had so many people praying for us: we felt wrapped in a halo of prayers, and priesthood, and temple rolls. These above all carried us through the times when the prognosis was not promising. When the radiation failed to slow the tumor, I knew the Lord was going to give us Paul's "far better" rather than his "more needful," and Laurie's "gain" would be my loss. Yet the hopes still rose and fell, as constant as the swell of the ocean waves. At night the winds quickened and the troughs and peaks lifted and dropped with sudden motion.

INCOMPLETE MASTERPIECE

One has to fight the sense of incompleteness, of time unfulfilled, of missions unaccomplished—the Mount Nebo views. The clay on the potter's wheel still needs some turning and shaping. "She is only fifty-six!" I told God. She turned fifty-seven less than two months before her death. After the chemotherapy drained so much remaining life out of her, I told her I could not give her those horrible pills again, and we turned ourselves completely over to the mercies of the Lord. We decided to go ahead and travel to Italy, our favorite country in Europe, even though she was weak. Laurie loved the art of Florence. She had studied it and come to know it intimately. My daughter and I pushed her in the wheelchair from place to place and let her look at the treasures of the Renaissance: Ghiberti's *Doors*, Giotto's *Tower*, Brunelleschi's *Dome*, Michelangelo's *David*.

But I knew the one place above all she would want to

visit. We rattled her down the cobblestone streets to the Bargello Museum, which houses the *Pitti Tondo* carved by Michelangelo. It is a small round sculpture of the Madonna and young Jesus. Years earlier, Laurie had sung "Mary's Lullaby" in front of it and brought everyone in the room to tears, including our Italian host, who could not continue guiding us through the collection. She had begun to draw it as a Christmas present for the children. She labored over every detail, but it never lived up to her sense of perfection, so Christmas after Christmas would pass while the art remained incomplete. I used to prod her to finish it, but to no avail. As she began to weaken with the cancer, I found the drawing and had it framed, telling her, "I asked them to leave the back open so if you want you can finish it." Now, in Florence, as she sat in front of the one piece of art she loved best, I noticed that it too was unfinished—and in the exact same places as her framed drawing hanging on the wall back home. It seemed the symbol of her life—already so beautiful, a masterpiece, but wanting the sculptor to return for those final soft hammer blows that would make elegance perfection. Not to be. Not in this life.

WAITING

The impatience of grief became our constant acquaintance. It seemed we were always waiting—for the next appointment, the next MRI, results from the radiation, when to go on steroids. Would we be able to go to

Normandy, a long-held wish of Laurie's? Could we take the kids to Peru, which was her last deep desire, her holding on to the old life and the cherished dreams we had planned? How fast would the cancer invade the healthy tissues and cause further deterioration of her abilities? Which would go next: sight, movement, memory? Would she ever recover her speech after the chemotherapy compromised it so dramatically? It is still so hard to push out of my mind her questioning plea, "When is it going to come back?"

Then there was the last awful waiting of which we never spoke because she could not make herself believe it was really coming and because I pushed its inevitability into a more distant future. With what growing anxiety my children and I watched her actions: biting into an orange with the peel still on it, washing darks with whites and staining them all yellow, trying desperately to turn down the volume on the television when it was the radio in the room that was blaring, falling twice on the airplane and getting wedged between the seats, dragging her right foot more and more, struggling to make our queen-size bed with three twin sheets. There was increasing confusion at each meal as she began eating with a knife instead of a fork and finally her fingers. Here was this most feminine of women fighting to keep her independence by applying makeup with a shaking hand and curling what little remained of her hair. Laurie's hair was a merry stream descending from high mountains. I could drown my hands in the clean, clear-rinsing flow of it. Even that she lost. Could not the cancer leave her a small gracing of beauty, grant her at least one last touch of femininity, of dignity? Could it not leave a little of Laurie in Laurie?

How she scolded, with her eyes and incomprehensible speech, my daughter and me for bringing the hospice bed into the family room—and yet how meekly she climbed into it moments later. At the end there was the relief of morphine, the creeping immobility, the complete locking of the muscles in her face, which became as hard as stone, then coma. Why did death have to creep up on her like a coward, hiding behind every tree in the forest but somehow having drawn nearer each time we looked? Yet release arrived, and death became her friend. The slow-plodding, downward-drawing wait was over, peace from pain, joy obtained, lessons learned, school out, holidays begun.

Now I wait—and try to live with grief's impatient expectations for early releases. When will life become normal? What *is* "normal" anymore? When will the pain subside—or will it? Do I even wish it to? Would it indicate a diminishing of my love? How long before weeping becomes merely tears? If my Eden is gone, there must be joys in the lone world; it cannot be all dreary. I must not allow it to become such. For the happiness that is still to be found outside the boundary guarded by the flaming sword I must wait and search. It is easy now to feel why Adam left Eden: not so much to fulfill some premortal doctrinal plan of which he had small understanding, but to remain with Eve—the woman he loved. God relied on their love for each other, not only on the hope of eternal progression or future knowledge—on the heart rather than the mind. When God asked him what he had done, Adam spoke of Eve, not of the need to multiply the earth (see Genesis 3:9–12).

MY RACHEL

Of course there is and always will be the hardest waiting of all—that of reunion. But here God has helped me. So many times I have read the story of Jacob and Rachel and found within it a mirror for my own love for Laurie. I have taught this very personal context more times than I can count. With all respect to Shakespeare, Austen, and all the other great authors, there is no love story in literature that can match that of Jacob and Rachel, and I have favored it since my youth.

"Shouldest thou . . . serve me for nought? tell me, what shall thy wages be?" Laban asked Jacob, who knew exactly what was worth laboring for. "Rachel was beautiful and well favoured. And Jacob loved Rachel." He more than knew her value, and answered, "I will serve thee seven years for Rachel thy younger daughter" (Genesis 29:15–18). I often wonder what Rachel thought during those seven years, as season by season she watched Jacob working with the flocks—knowing that every hour, every day was all for her. Seven long years!

A side note: I have been reflecting on a statement by Wilford Woodruff, who taught the men of his generation: "If you lived here in the flesh a thousand years . . . and labored all your life in poverty, and when you got through, if, by your acts, you could secure your wives and children in the morning of the first resurrection, to dwell with you in the presence of God, that one thing would amply pay you for the labors of a thousand years" (in *Journal of Discourses*, 21:284).

Laban accepted Jacob's seven-year offer, telling him, "It is better that I give her to thee, than that I should give her to another man: abide with me" (Genesis 29:19). These words I have repeated to myself a thousand times over the last few months. Laurie told me soon after we were married how she came to her decision to say yes to my so, so very early proposal. We had dated only six weeks, and she had just turned eighteen (but then, Jacob asked for Rachel after only a month of knowing her). "God told me I would be making a mistake if I said no!" Laurie explained. It is crucial for me to believe that God, Laurie's Father, speaks to me Laban's words and will continue with his conclusion.

Laban finished with the words, "abide with me." There is the key phrase! As my Father in Heaven offers me the same invitation, I will now labor for my eternal bride. I must "abide" with the Lord, the Eternal Father of Laurie, and work out my "seven years' wait."

The story of Jacob's seven years of service for Rachel ends with what is surely the most romantic sentence in all literature, more powerful because the sentiment and the story are true. "And they seemed unto him but a few days, for the love he had to her" (Genesis 29:20). Therein is my hope and my deliverance from waiting. Whatever time is remaining to me on earth, however long I must endure, I will abide with and labor for the Lord. Whatever He wants from me, I will give Him. There is a sweet release in consecration, a quiet letting go of the will in a single focus, a solitary desired blessing. Since the story of Jacob and Rachel is a true one, then for me also it will all seem like a few days. Then, at the sunset of my own life, at the ending of labors, I, like Jacob, will one day look toward my Heavenly Father and ask, "Give me my wife, for my days are fulfilled" (Genesis 29:21). The story has only increased in its power to inspire me by the added poignancy that Rachel died young and Jacob mourned for her all his life.

CHAPTER VII

SUNSET

. . . I love thee with the breath,
Smiles, tears, of all my life!—and, if God choose,
I shall but love thee better after death.

Sonnet Forty-Three

A Weeping Joy

*A*ll of the challenges became more bearable two nights after her death when the midnight thoughts were halted and made to retreat, though not banished from the field. On that night I first experienced the balm of a weeping joy. It really wasn't so profound an experience—quite simple, actually. It was just the thought growing into an assurance and finally lodging in my being that life's adversities were completed for Laurie. She had reached the ending place. By that I did not mean just the eight months of cancer, but all the pain she had fought during the last ten years of her life; it meant what we refer to as the testing or proving of mortality. She was free of it all. As Jesus on the cross said of the pains and purposes of His life, "It is finished" (John 19:30), so too was it finished for my Laurie. She had endured enough pain in mortality to enjoy more deeply the happiness and rest of eternity. I pray she will experience as much joy as her merry heart can feel.

Gratitude swept over me, into me, all around me, and I wept for the first time with joy, joy at her release. I felt myself smiling again. It was over, all of it was over! How wonderful for her! For the time I was not conscious of my own hurting. I don't recall ever feeling such joy in another's happiness. My pain was swallowed up in gladness for her. She mattered most of all; for the moment I was inconsequential. It was that "gush of compassion," that swelling of selfless love a beloved Hindu parable contained which I had frequently taught. It was a taste of the Buddha's "Nirvana," the state where pain is ended in the total outward vision of the soul that feels only for others, not for self. It was Christianity's definition of charity, the love that "seeketh not her own" (1 Corinthians 13:5). It was insight into the pure love of Christ, and how soothing to an aching soul it was. I wept as hard that night as I had ever wept in grief. How happy I was for her! I thanked God for ending her trials and accepting her into His own care. It was not as hard knowing she was passing into His guardianship. I could let her go.

The feeling lasted throughout the night, and for the first time since that awful April day, the midnight stirrings had to hide from the light of compassionate, selfless joy. I knew at that same moment that she would also want me to be cheerful and to delight in the relationships and experiences that were left to me in life. I cannot always bring back the weeping joy, but the memory of how I felt that night, the emotion of it all, as well as the reasoning, can still hold at bay the night thoughts. I still weep for the loss of her touch, her voice, her presence, but at least now there is a smile behind the tears, one that remains with me, as constant a companion and comforter as the Holy Spirit. Maybe it is the Holy Spirit.

CHRISTMAS 1971, CHRISTMAS 2010

A friend told me that in time I would forget the painful scenes of Laurie's last months, weeks, and final days. Of this I have no doubt, for I have no desire to remember Laurie as she was during those times. I do not wish to suffer twice, once in reality and then again in retrospect. She is not that way now. To help me distance myself from them, I have spent days returning to the places where we shared some of our most cherished times. It helps to push back the cancer days so they don't so dominate my field of vision.

We met and began dating during Thanksgiving and Christmas season 1971. I drove down to BYU one morning to retrace those earliest memories, the once-upon-a-time days, the princess-and-the-frog days. So much has changed. The Step Down Lounge of the Smith Family Living Center where our ward met is long gone, as is the old Joseph Smith building where we watched fifty-cent weekend movies early in our marriage because we could afford nothing else. The apartment complex where I picked her up for dates, filled with my nervous excitement, has been renamed and remodeled, but the little house we lived in during our married year at school still stands just as it did almost forty years ago. I walked the campus, breathing the chill winter air, and the pleasant, moving memories of the lovely long ago returned to shadow the harsher, more recent ones. As long as these live, she lives, and the "us" part of my being does not seem to be so distant.

You can't go back, I know, as much as I would like to, if only for a day or two, but something remains in those places so strongly attached to the emotions, something cleansing and joy producing. I have wondered if I have been living too much in the past lately, yet there are days when it seems that is all I have. The future, except the far-distant one, does not yet hold for me any great expectations. I pray for God's guidance and use of me. I do not view the future as a frightening, or a sorrowful, or a lonely place, just a location without dimensions, open, without borders, mist-filled, fog-shrouded, a neutral, somewhat blank corner that fills me with confusion if I peer into it too closely. I know that may change. I'll need to "move on," but for the present time, the past appears as the loveliest place to dwell.

I wanted to give Laurie a gift for Christmas that would somehow bring all my feelings for her together in one final assurance of her place in my life. By early December we knew the time was short as she was changing daily. What do you give a dying spouse, your best friend?

Thirty-nine Christmases ago, after we had dated for only a few weeks, I sent her my first Christmas present. Actually, it was the first thing I ever gave her. We had both gone home for the holidays, me to California and Laurie to Canada. She loved Winnie the Pooh, so I bought her a stuffed "Pooh Bear," then debated if I should include the Chanel #5 I had bought in France during my mission. By then, however, I had no doubts that she was the girl I wanted, so I risked it all and placed the perfume in the bear's paws with a brief note: "I brought this perfume back with me from France and have been saving it for someone special. You're that someone." I'm sure I terrified both her parents that Christmas morning. Of her own emotions I never asked her.

The note and the bear she saved throughout the years in a plastic bag because the seams had separated and the stuffing was spilling out. On this last Christmas, with my daughter's help, we found a duplicate "Pooh" and wrapped Chanel #5 once again in his paws with a tiny note attached. "You still are and forever will be that someone special." I wanted so badly for her to understand, to recall the Christmas of 1971, to receive the gift within the gift, but her mind was so invaded by the cancer that we could be certain of nothing. I gave it to her four days before Christmas. Did she remember? Did she make the connection?

I could not be sure. But if the spirit remembers and records everything, then by now she knows. A concerned friend wrote to me the words I most needed to hear at that uncertain time:

"Laurie's spirit is soaking in every act, every expression of love, every important moment with you and her

children and grandchildren—to not only relive again and again but to have constantly before her when she steps across the veil and time is suddenly different, but all of the love, the bonds, the covenants between the two of you and throughout your family are not only the same, but, I am guessing, enhanced by her new surroundings."

God so often speaks to us through our friends. I believe these words to be true, so now a second bear sits next to the original in its accustomed place on the shelf.

THE GLORIES OF THE DAY

The last tour I had taken with Laurie was to Peru in October. I had flown to South America a week early to be with another group but would meet Laurie in Lima. That morning I watched the sun rise over Lake Titicaca high in the Andes. It was one of the most beautiful sunrises I had ever seen. The surface of the lake was smooth, and in the clear, high air I could see far into the distance beyond the reeds and islands. I thought about how delightful the morning was, so alive with anticipation, so bright and welcoming. Beginnings are such lovely things, so full of promise and hope.

That evening I flew along the Pacific coast as the sun set over the ocean. I know I have never witnessed a more magnificent sunset in all my life. It lasted for nearly an hour, a gift from a gracious Father in Heaven, perhaps made more splendid because at that moment I so needed hope and joy. The clouds reflected all the colors of the spectrum. The hues went from the lightest shades of pink, coral, and orange to the deepest crimson. In the final moments, the scarlet sky at the horizon shone bright against the now-black clouds, which did not fight the glow but enhanced it. Above, in the azure blue of a deepening night, a tiny sliver of a moon cradled Venus. I thought: "How lovely is a sunset." As I watched the last threads of light diminish, the Lord spoke to my heart, and divine healing surrounded me.

> *Sunsets are beautiful things!*
> *Endings as well as beginnings!*
> *They do not plunge the world into darkness,*
> *But remind us of the glories of the day,*
> *And the promise that the sun will rise again.*

Only when the sun sets do we know how warm and wonderful it is and how its light has touched everything upon which it shines. It brings rich, vibrant, joyful life. Love is like that. Was there any part of me she did not touch? Was there any shadow she could not lighten? So it is not into darkness of grief I go, but into the brightness of remembered joys, all the treasured, tiny happinesses that Laurie gave to me, shared with me, created with me during our lives together. And as she is forgiving, all my faults will melt away through the warmth of her grace, and remembered pains will be forgotten. We all have the promise, in all of our loves, that the sun will rise again in our hearts, for there are wondrous embracings awaiting us. It is just behind an opening door, through the rustling of a parting curtain, at the scented end of the flower, in the light around the earth's turning where we will receive the best gifts our God and Savior have to bestow.

At this moment Laurie is happy, young, vital, filled with life and energy, walking and speaking and singing without impediments, overflowing with luminous joy. I believe she will shine some down upon me. I can see her through my soul's eyes, and if she will wait for me and love me still, then the intervening years I may be without her will truly be as those seven years were to Jacob as he labored for his beloved Rachel, "but a few days." I will be in heaven already. Ultimately, I will have never lived anywhere else.

In the meantime, God has given me His first expectation. It is not a difficult one, but one that must be done thoroughly and with no looking back. It is a housecleaning akin to the one I must soon begin in the closets and drawers of our home with Laurie's things. It is the cleansing of the spirit, and the mind, and the heart, of every unhelpful, disapproving, painful, or harmful moment, thought, word, or act in the years of our friendship and shared life together—all of hers, all of mine. It is a courteous clearing away of all the mental clutter that might have accumulated over the years, leaving only kindness, warmth, and mercy in the memory. It is a gentle bathing of remembrance, a last baptism, which removes all past imperfections, frailties, or hurts that may hide within the soul and harbor, though ever so small, any unfavorable or judgmental vision of this woman with whom I shared so much of life and whom I knew so well. All is past and may now be graciously and kindly discarded and forgotten, not just forgiven. We are the sum total of all our goodness, all our positives. The deficiencies, the minuses, because they are negative are less than zero—less than nothing—and so they simply pass away, ciphers needing no recognition. That is a dying that is life-giving, the best death one can know.

"Help us, Father, to remove everything those we love would not wish to remain in our hearts, everything that would give them embarrassment, discomfort, or pain."

We would not devote any corner of our souls for such things; there is room enough only for love and kindness. "You must leave all the 'motes and beams' at the door of heaven," the Lord tells us. "There is no place for them here."

In the sorting and ordering of the corners and closets of the soul, there will be many things to treasure and reflect upon. All the goodness, the laughter, the holiness, the sacrifice and loving will be held foremost in our spirits. I will think only of Laurie in the highest flowering of her becoming. She is the crowning culmination of all her righteousness from every moment of her life. This is what the Lord anticipates. This is how He sees. It is what all must do, whichever side of the veil we may be on when separation comes. How refreshing and healing it is just to let things go, to sweep the soul pure of the motes and beams of accruing years! How joyous and renewing to visit again and again the sweetness of the heart's past kind giving—to block out every flaw. Yes, even to clothe reality in memory's softest colors and make it more beautiful.

"FOREVER WILT THOU LOVE . . ."

The challenge of writing about life-changing encounters is knowing when to cease. I fear to write or refine much more lest the emotion become contrived or sincerity compromised. I so earnestly desire honesty. Everything still floats so near the surface of my heart, yet the time may soon come when the learning sinks into the depths of memory and drawing it upwards again with clarity becomes too difficult a labor. The journey we began that April night can only end with behind-the-veil redresses. It goes on, as life must go on and move forward with "brightness of hope." Grief has become my companion, though not entirely unwelcome, for he carves the hollow that one day love and Laurie will fill with joy. If the wound be deep, the balm that heals it will be all the sweeter. Then will come that yearning, enduring gratitude to our God whose concern for these human hearts of ours found a way.

I know there will be difficult days ahead. For the time being, I am running, through the busyness of my life and constant occupation of my time, to stay one reach ahead of grief's most fatal footfalls. I must go through her things soon, and decisions will be made. The dress she wore on

those magic nights I will keep with its whisper of perfume.
Her hairbrush with a few long strands still caught within its
bristles, the pencils she drew with, the music she sang in the
Holy Land, pieces of oft-worn jewelry, the golden navigator's
compass she gave me one Christmas, and the books with her
underlinings or straying pen marks will stay with me. And,
of course, there are the pictures and the notes and cards in
which I can still hear her voice. All these, and others I shall
discover in the awaiting days, will bring the poignant, sweet
aching of memory. All who grieve will keep those things that
draw the beloved's presence nearer. They are healing. They
increase as well as maintain the bond. They will be different
for each of us, and the simplest object may bring the stron-
gest ties.

I struggled hard with the decision, but ended up keep-
ing her wedding ring. There was a certain stab of nostalgia
in removing it. I hope I made the right choice. The inscrip-
tion we placed in hers is coupled with the one in mine, and
I could not see it go into the ground. It is a line from Keats
that I had the good fortune to be studying when I proposed:
"Forever wilt thou love, and she be fair." I could not have
imagined when I had the first four words of that verse en-
graved in my ring and the last four in hers how appropriate
they would remain and the smile they would bring in our
current parting. She is fairer now than she ever was in life,
and my love will certainly be forever. She lost her contact
lens the night I gave the ring to her, and we spent fifteen
minutes looking for it before she could see her diamond

and read the engravings. How often did we laugh over that memory!

I will face the first year's difficult anniversaries—which may not become less tender or sore with the accumulation of successive years, yet the joyful ones must remain joyful and not sink into loneliness. Our wedding day was the happiest moment of my life and so it will remain. I will continue to ask myself, "Where are you now, Laurie? What are you doing today? How do you feel? What are you thinking? What memories bless you or haunt you? The last I pray you forget. Can you hear me when I talk to you? I tell you I love you every day and all that you mean to me. Is your love growing for me as mine is for you?" I will continue to talk to her with the same casual reverence of whispered prayer, sometimes shifting from my Father in Heaven to Laurie and back again in mid conversation. I don't suppose the Lord minds such intimate sharing or lovely company. If she can't receive my words, I ask God, who can, to tell her all I feel.

> *"Tell her, Lord, that she was the loveliest thing my eyes ever rested upon, that the greatest happinesses of my life were centered in her. She was my best friend, and I will always love her."*

Even the smallest actions or memories may surprise us with their pull. I shall not forget the first time I returned to the house and the truth struck me like a blow that she was not there. I will walk those places we dreamed of visiting together and listen for a footstep or change in the breeze to let me know she is with me if only fleetingly, longing to hear again the excitement in her voice: "Who would have thought that a small-town Alberta girl would be standing here!"

I will know her loss in the faces of my children and grandchildren and in the voices of her friends. The unexpected and unaccounted for will surely come, leaving me, at least initially, with no defenses. Rising sorrow will break once again into sobbing or quiet tears. How it stung to circle the "w" for widower on an entry visa less than two weeks after her death, or to receive four days after the funeral a well-intentioned invitation in the mail to attend a singles' activity for those widowed, or to hear a good friend say—I'm sure meaning it consolingly—"Of course, you'll remarry." Does not the ring I wear on my finger with its four cherished words tell me I am still married? And I've never said good-bye.

Hearing: "Only one?" or "Just you?" when checking in for a flight or being seated at a restaurant will never feel normal. It's as if others are as surprised as I am that Laurie is not standing next to me. I no longer carry her passport, or help her search for her sunglasses, or place her feet on the rests of the wheelchair, or make her eggs and orange juice for breakfast—but I wake to her picture on the nightstand by my bed, the first thing I greet each morning.

There are the bright spots, too. Her hand remained quite warm in mine right up to the last gentle breaths. There was no creeping chill. The beautiful music and thoughts shared at her funeral and the continual pouring out of love by so many concerned friends stay soft and comforting. I discovered anew the last note she wrote me with its broken thoughts and apologetic tone—"I'm sorry to go by Kirsten's today but I'm got to play for by myself . . ."—because she drove the car when she knew her medical condition forbade it. But she ended the note with, "I love you, and I'll be back. All my love, Laurie." I thank God that the cancer could not confuse *that* message. Comfort on a scrap of paper!

There was the dreaded next-day visit to the cemetery, yet I found her grave covered with hundreds of flowers, unwilted, frozen fresh in their spring colors with the white frost of the mountains reflecting the winter sun. The gift of friends! Here was a touch of May on a January morning. Warm memories and even laughter are surfacing in the drawers and closets that contained what she gathered and saved over the years. She rarely threw anything away and was often afraid I would. There are little notes with exclamation points following them stating emphatically, "DON'T THROW AWAY!"

I have felt her passing draw my children closer into my heart, and friends have become dearer to me. It has also been a long time since prayer has meant so much or the temple been such a necessity. We must learn to meet the good and the bad, the tender and the remorse-filled moments day by day as they come. We do not face them all at once. Both are expressions of our love.

LIGHTING THE HEART FOREVER

*A*s I ponder on the possibility of future light, another memory unfolds. Early in December we had made our last trip. It was to Wichita to see our son, daughter-in-law, and grandchildren. Laurie was declining daily by this time. The flights were a surreal nightmare, but I'm glad we did it. Our four-year-old grandson was so very tender with her, sitting on her lap for wheelchair rides and lying next to her on the couch for naps. Precious memories! We celebrated Christmas early and I gave my son two pictures of his mother so he would remember her as she was when he was growing up. He also opened the last present Laurie had chosen for her children, handmade Christmas tree decorations, individually selected for each child in Rothenberg, Germany, that July. The atmosphere became heavy with love, and many tears were shed. My grandson sat quietly on the floor next to the Christmas tree watching all the adults weeping around him. Suddenly he stood up and called to us all, "Hey, everybody! It's Christmas!"

It is good to be reminded of reasons we have to rejoice, especially when surrounded by our trials. Our Father in Heaven desires our happiness. We believe in a gospel of joy, of good news, of gladness. My grandson's so very appropriate reminder will linger forever in my soul. Each day of the coming years will always be Christmas, for "in thy dark streets shineth The everlasting Light" (*Hymns*, no. 208). Laurie and I are encircled within that light. Sunsets *can* be glorious.

CHAPTER VIII

COMPENSATORY GRACES

Thou comest! All is said without a word.
I sit beneath thy looks, as children do
In the noon-sun . . .

Sonnet Thirty-One

RACHEL'S TOMB

*I*t has been more than two months since I wrote the previous chapter, but I knew I would write one more—one that would allow for the passage of a small amount of time and the perspective it might grant me. It would also allow a visit to Rachel's Tomb in the Holy Land. I don't know when the urgency to visit the tomb began, but it mounted during those intense grieving days to the level of an obsessive hope. I had to go to the tomb. Laurie had always been "my Rachel," and I had told the Lord that all the days of my remaining life were His. I have not felt so consecrated before. I would feed His flocks, laboring for Him—and for her.

I had never been to the tomb, a small, domed, white limestone building with arches so typical of the area. But I had passed it many times on our way to Bethlehem, where I took tour groups to the Church of the Nativity, then into the intimate little cloister where Laurie had always led them in singing Christmas carols before she sang "Mary's Lullaby" to them.

Being in the area brought back the memory of the last time I had heard that song: in July, while on an airplane coming home from Germany. Laurie was listening to music our children had prepared for her on an iPod. I looked at her and could see she was deeply moved by something. She didn't say a word, just removed one of the earphones and placed it in my ear, then played for me "Mary's Lullaby." I wasn't sure why she wanted me to hear this particular song, as we were nowhere near Bethlehem or Christmas, but I understood when I heard the words, "Away, spectered future of sorrow and plight. Away to the years that must follow tonight" (Bertha A. Kleinman, published by Wanda West Palmer, Mesa, Arizona).

Now I was again in Bethlehem, but without her. I breathed in the memories, then left the group and took a private car to Rachel's Tomb. I don't know what I expected: miracles, I suppose, her voice in my heart, a sense of her total forgiveness for my many failings, the feel of her standing by my side, a whispered, "I still love you, Mike." My hopes were so high.

Security issues in Israel had dramatically changed Rachel's Tomb from the setting I remembered. The towering, bleak-concrete security wall built around the West Bank ran just a few feet next to the tomb. It was enclosed now, cut off from the sun and contained within its own walls in bunker fashion. We drove down the canyon of grey concrete and parked the car. I took my scriptures, already feeling the disappointment, and passed the security check. Construction was continuing, and the sound of pounding jackhammers rang through the hallway leading to the cenotaph that marked the traditional spot where Jacob set up a pillar in memorial of his beloved Rachel. Orthodox Jews crowded the remaining space around the tomb, and there was barely room for me to pass. The tomb was draped in a black velvet cloth with Hebrew letters that I could not read. It was covered in dust from all the construction. I found a corner and read the twenty-ninth chapter of Genesis, desperately hoping that God would not let me down, but nothing came.

In time I closed my Bible and walked out, wondering why I had felt so compelled to visit this place and feeling as discouraged as I had been in a long time. I had bent all my energies to this moment. What would I look forward to now?

I returned to the small open square next to where my car and driver were waiting with my guide when I saw that someone had planted a tiny spot of garden in the corner. It was the only sign of beauty and life in the midst of all that dead and barren cement and asphalt. I was drawn to it. There on the wall above the blooming flowers of an Israeli spring were the words of Jeremiah, written by the grieving prophet at the loss of his people. I read the words:

"Thus saith the Lord; A voice was heard in Ramah, lamentation, and bitter weeping; Rahel weeping for her

*children refused to be comforted for her children, because
they were not.*

*"Thus saith the Lord; Refrain thy voice from weep-
ing, and thine eyes from tears: for thy work shall be rewarded, saith the Lord; and they shall come again. . . .*

"And there is hope in thine end, saith the Lord."

JEREMIAH 31:15—17

Joseph, my guide and good friend, seeing how moved I
was, quietly said, "Those are the words written on Rachel's
Tomb."

God had not failed me. It was how most of my answers
from Him have come. Why is our Father in Heaven so infi-
nitely good to us sometimes? Was He not assuring me that
He will accept my labors and my Rachel will be mine again?
"Thy work shall be rewarded. . . . There is hope in thine
end." I can let the fears go. "Thus saith the Lord." A single
eternity of gratitude and adoration will not be sufficient for
my indebtedness to Him. I will need two—one for His eternal kindnesses bestowed from before my birth, and one for
Laurie.

We left the tomb and Joseph took me to Ramat Rahel,
Rachel's Hill, the place spoken of by Jeremiah. We climbed
to the top, and the beautiful green hills of Judea spread before us. I could see Bethlehem to the south, the place of our
Savior's birth with its promise of hope, and Jerusalem in
the distance to the north, the place of His Resurrection and
even greater hope. Below us lay the road. Somewhere along

that stretch of valleys and hills, Rachel died and was buried. She is surrounded by the bookends of the grace of Christ, enfolded within the boundaries of his mortal life and sacrifice of mercy—as is my Laurie—as are we all.

THE LETTERS

*T*he Lord's and Laurie's goodness did not end on the road to Bethlehem. Since her death I had often and fervently wished I could just have a letter from her, something I could always carry with me to read and reread—one that would let me share her mind and know how she was doing and how she felt. How comfortable it would feel folded and waiting in my pocket or in the desk drawer. I had spoken of this desire, but with wishing known only in a fantasy. There are no letters from heaven; the spirit world has no mail service.

I spent four weeks clearing out the house, from the upstairs bedroom to the closets in the basement. I found a shoe box with the dried remains of two dozen roses I had given her on a special anniversary. They looked so fragile lying there, the fragrance gone, with only memory clinging to them. After her passing, I had bought her a dozen red roses for Valentine's Day. I thought I would take them to the cemetery, but I didn't have the heart to turn onto the side road that led to her grave. I never picture her as being there anyway. I drove home and arranged them instead in one of her crystal vases and put them between her pictures on the dresser in the bedroom. They stayed fresh and cheered the room for nearly two weeks, a lovely sign of enduring life and lasting spring. I've determined that all the flowers of the future will be given to the eighteen-year-old girl I fell in love with, whose photograph rests on the dresser, and not to the grass by a headstone. There is something too final about that piece of granite that I cannot relate to my Laurie. It draws upward the good-bye I cannot give. I pray that somehow I can still contribute to her happiness, to bring a smile to her face even if I cannot see it. Flowers had always been such a simple way of doing it. And I gave too few.

One of the last things I discovered in going through the house was her worn and scarred old pink suitcase stored in the fruit room. The locks and hinges were broken and the contents were pushing out, but I could see that everything had once been organized neatly and laid in carefully. Here were pictures and cutouts she had used as Junior Primary chorister before she went to college, awards and report cards from high school, conservatory scores and music from piano recitals, pictures of friends and family, and Mother's Day cards from the children when they were young. In one corner, under some music, I found a bundle of eight letters addressed to:

Mr. Michael Wilcox
3323 Mayfield
San Bernardino, California

Laurie had written them in the spring and summer of 1972 during our engagement while I was working in

California and she was in Canada preparing for our July wedding. Lying next to them were my letters to her written at the same time. I stared at the miracle of them, then finally reached for them and held them in my hand for the longest time. I had forgotten they even existed. I had no memory of what they contained. I didn't open them, but waited until everyone was gone from the house and I was alone. I couldn't read them all at one sitting—it would have seemed irreverent, somehow unhallowed, indulgent—so I read one letter each night for eight nights, then started over again for another eight nights. I also read those I had sent her in Canada. Her letters were so much more mature than mine although I was four years older, had served a mission, and was an English major and an aspiring writer.

Is it possible in God's wisdom, where all things are seen in the present, that an eighteen-year-old girl occupied with wedding dresses, bridesmaids, centerpieces, receptions, and bridal showers could be inspired to write—with maturity beyond her experience—the very words her husband would need four decades in the future when he was sixty-one and mourning her passing? Since her death I had only been able to imagine her as the girl who had enchanted me so thoroughly—not the girl of my dreams, but the girl beyond my dreams—and now, here were the words of that young woman. She spoke to my fears and my doubts.

I had thrashed and harvested my regrets until they were winnowed and ground down and had dusted with guilt the insides of my soul. All my heaven-sent penance would not ease the growing fields of my "I should haves." Yet I opened the envelope and read:

> "Please don't apologize for those few bad moments. We both learned a lot from them. We still have a lot to learn, but learning is a joy, especially when it is shared. Life won't always be easy for us, as we both know. We've got a lot of weeds to pull and rocks to throw out of our way yet, but, darling, if we stay together through it all and with the Lord guiding our way, I know with all my heart that we can stand up to everything. I love you so much for all you are to me. Please always remember that I need you beside me forever and eternity. Love, Laurie."

I had a good fresh cry with those words. It was so cleansing. The intensity her death had given to my love came anew, and to feel love at that deep level is to know a joy through the grieving.

Walking into the Rainbow

God is teaching me that I can come near to Laurie in the beauty and silence of purer creation. I have spent so much time and anxiety waiting for her to approach me, thinking this was how it had to be, everything in her and God's control, but in silent, beautiful places I seem to enter her world and feel enclosed somehow in her heart and mind. It is difficult to describe. You can't touch the rain, but you can let it touch you if you go out into it. Sometimes it feels like a tiny sun is shining, not outside down, but inside outwards. Sometimes in the grand quiet of southern Utah where we frequently hiked I step into her thoughts, into her love. I feel like I'm walking toward a rainbow that does not recede with my approach, moving forward until there is a washing away of sadness in a waterfall of color—or into the Milky Way's cascading splash of stars at the night's horizon. Silence and beauty! Certainly they are the elements of her spirit world, the things her mind is focused on. At times, when I walk in those beautiful creations where you can hear the silence itself, not slight sounds within the silence, I seem to meet her, and the coming together is so casual, as if she turned, not in surprise, and said, "Oh, so you're here too." When I feel I have entered her thoughts I can almost see her dawning awareness, as if she looked up from some eternal lesson, found me near, and smiled.

It is difficult, even in these settings, to quiet the mind down. Mine is always so busy searching for things to think, for memories to sort through or improvements to be made in myself, and far too often when I think of her my inadequacies come rushing in and disturb the calm. I keep throwing rocks through the surface of the lake, and the surrounding reflections are harder to see. I'm trying to learn to be quiet internally. I read her words and the surface becomes smooth again.

"You've asked me before, 'Are you mine?' and I'll tell you again. Yes, yes, and yes. I'm yours forever."

I hiked one morning among towering walls of red stone and felt so close to her I could almost see her sitting on the cliff top with her knees drawn up and her arms locked around them. She always loved the view from the peak and had climbed more mountains than I can remember. I had once asked her when she first thought she was in love with me. She said, "It was on a November evening when I came to the window of my apartment and saw you walking across the parking lot below, alone and deep in thought as the snow was falling. 'This is a good man,' I thought, 'I can entrust my heart to him.'" Now as I walked, feeling her eyes on me and my own obvious inadequacies, her words floated down and calmed again the widening ripples of my mind. "I still see that good man walking in the snow, lost in thought." A quiet mind in a quiet place has become a central concern now.

DREAM WITHOUT WORDS

I would wait through the day knowing another letter was resting on the nightstand. The hours seemed to glide more softly along throughout the morning and afternoon, and when evening came and the house was quiet, I would read her words.

"You are all I have ever wanted and searched for. Soon you will be mine. I pray I may be worthy of your love and protection. I look to you so much and I hope I won't demand too much from you. Sometimes, I think I

can't go another minute if you don't come up to me and give me a hug. But I do. I love you so very much. Please always remember this. I want to be your wife and companion forever. "

One's hunger is never satisfied, the thirst never quenched. I fear too frequently I have gone to the Lord and said,

"Again, please, Father, again, for the sake of my Thomas heart."

Could she hear me when I spoke to her between the lines of her letters? I often petitioned the Lord, *"Can I not have just one dream about Laurie?"* I wanted something to go with her letters, something with the reality dreams so often bestow, images as well as words, a filling of the senses, a touch, a voice. She had to know how much I loved her, and I could not send her a letter in return.

I had spent the day wandering a primitive area in one of the national parks and my soul was calm. Yet I had a terrible nightmare, one of the worst of my life, and awoke in fear. *"Let me have just one dream, Father, one sweet dream, please!"* It was halfway between a plea and a demand, but I had made it so many times before.

Slipping back into sleep, I found myself sitting next to Laurie traveling to some unknown destination. Everything seemed so natural. She was quiet, pensive, hesitant, and looked away as if distracted. "Do you still love me?" she finally said. I would have anticipated that such a question should have come from me. I said nothing this time, being usually too full of words, but held her in my arms for the longest time. She put her head next to mine. I could feel her hair touching my face. There was no sorrow, just her sitting next to me, close, touching. We stopped at a river and began walking down its bank, I on one side and she on the other, walking parallel, with her a little ahead of me. For some reason the river's separation did not seem unnatural. I took my eyes off her for an instant to glance into the running water, and when I looked up she was gone. There must be a crossing at the end of the dream farther up the river with her waiting at the ford. I awoke and felt an urgency to draw the memory from my sleeping mind to my waking one lest I lose the Lord's gift. I realized in the morning that I never answered her question, and my need for words was too strong. I returned to the canyon I had hiked the previous day and cried up to the cliffs, "More now than ever, Laurie!"

THE LAST LETTER

*I*t has been several months, and people ask me how I'm doing. I never quite know how to answer their question. It is always asked with sincere concern, and I so want to ease it. Often it feels like my life begins and ends with her, my essential life, anyway. The world was brighter, more beautiful, more vitally alive because she was in it. With her came dawn, the previous night of my life only noticed as twilight because she arose over the horizon. A close friend told me, "She tried in every way to be the foundation from which you could soar."

There is an unreal quality to the life I live now, a new dimension in which I am too aware of my surroundings. Perhaps it will pass, but for the present I feel as if I am somehow pretending to live. I'm on a stage in someone else's play. I have my stage life. I act out my roles. I interact with the other players. I say my lines and execute my entrances and exits. It's a good play, certainly not a tragedy, and the scenes are filled with wonderful people and much joy, even laughter. But the genuine life, the larger life, the loving life is somewhere else. There is an audience that watches; I can't see them in the darkness, but I sense their presence, their intense interest, and I strain to see those spiritual spectators— one in particular, one face, to hear one applause, to feel only one person's approval. I keep waiting for that moment when the lights will go down and I'll walk off the stage so my true life can continue. The audience will depart, the other players will go home, the crowds will thin, and I'll see her waiting in the wings. We'll walk off together, Laurie and I, and have toast and hot chocolate in the kitchen.

I opened the last letter with a sense of apprehension. They had been my lifeline, my connection to her; the catalyst that had brought so many mercies. Maybe it was the combination of the letters with the beauty of my surroundings that brought her so near.

"It was so good to hear from you yesterday and just to know that you still love me. I knew again that you were the one I needed so much to complete my life. I'm sorry I couldn't control my voice very well, but then I'm a woman and that's a good enough excuse. I miss you so terribly sometimes that I think I just can't go on. I need you to be there always and I know that you will be there; otherwise I just couldn't survive these past weeks or the ones ahead. Be a good boy. Laurie."

COMPENSATORY GRACES

When I think of the past weeks and months of my life with their pains and mercies, I marvel at the goodness God has shown to me. Amidst all my doubts, questions, and fears, He has not turned away, nor have I felt His disappointment with the wanderings of my faith. I have asked for too many "fleeces," like Gideon, and He has responded with understanding. I asked Him once why He was so patient and kind to me and received His answer.

"You were not granted your desired Hezekiah time. It is fitting that you should receive compensatory graces."

I sensed it was not just my answer but also Laurie's. Perhaps she received it long before my own mind had created the holding place to appreciate it. She so wanted to live, but I believe she too has received her compensatory graces, whatever they may be in that world in which she now walks. This is God's way, and He knows the right mercies to bestow on a hungering child denied hoped-for happinesses. Surely no man has more reason to rejoice than I.

A STOPPING PLACE

I know not the future windings of the road her loss may yet take me to, but I must find a stopping place because the path of grieving does not bring one to the dearly desired destination in this mortal life. Only earth-ending time can do that. Yet time, I am learning, intensifies our desires. It is a magnifying glass that focuses love like light in one concentrated burning ray upon a single soul—my Laurie's. It will be difficult to stop, for writing of Laurie has been a continued sharing of life and it feels a bit like losing her a second time, a certain thinning of my world. A wonderful Muslim friend of ours told me, "When we speak lovingly of those who have passed we lift them to higher and higher places in paradise." This is my lifting.

May this somewhat scattered chronicle of my own thoughts and feelings, written down in a pocket notebook throughout the months of my wife's and my encounter with cancer, her final passing, and its aftermath, help you with your own liftings. May it be a small permission for all to feel what they feel without wondering if they somehow lack faith or conviction or sufficient love—who question if what they are experiencing is normal, or healthy, or proper. I have been as open and honest and uncompromising with myself as I know how. Feeling is feeling, and for so many of us there arises that cry offered to Jesus two thousand years ago: "I believe; help thou mine unbelief" (Mark 9:24). That is the voice of humanity.

> "We mourn, Father; be with us in our mourning! Though thy scriptures so triumphantly ask, 'O death where is thy sting?' we know where to find it. We love, Father; help us in our loving. Teach us to walk the path that leads forward, into the arms of those we long for."

To those who know what it is to lament a dear one's passing—and ultimately that will be all of us who love—may that love be intensified, grounded on the bedrock of our deepest souls, and made holy by the separation. May you receive our Father's compensatory graces. May your sunsets be bright with time's remembered fullnesses. And during the dark hours, when the midnight thoughts turn in the mind, may the hope of an awaiting sunrise, on an eternal morning, light your hearts forever.

Until our own sunrise, Laurie, "little one," you will ever be serenely found within the circle of my being.

> "Michael, I'll keep you in my thoughts and my heart continually . . ."

And with God be the rest.

Sources

Frank, Anne. *The Diary of a Young Girl*. B.M. Mooyaart, trans. New York: Bantam Books, 1967.

Hymns of The Church of Jesus Christ of Latter-day Saints. Salt Lake City: The Church of Jesus Christ of Latter-day Saints, 1985.

Journal of Discourses. 26 vols. London: Latter-day Saints' Book Depot, 1854-56.

Lewis, C. S. *The Magician's Nephew*. New York: HarperCollins, 1983.

Nicholl, Charles. *Leonardo da Vinci: Flights of the Mind*. New York: Penguin Books, 2005.

Riffenburgh, Beau. *Shackleton's Forgotten Expedition: The Voyage of the Nimrod*. New York: Bloomsbury, 2005.

Thoreau, Henry David. *Walden and Other Writings*. New York: The Modern Library, 1950.

Note: The poetry excerpts that begin the chapters all come from Elizabeth Barrett Browning's *Sonnets from the Portuguese*, first published in 1850 and available today in numerous editions and online resources.